God's New Possibility

Cycle A Sermons for Advent, Christmas, and Epiphany Based on the Gospel Texts

James L. Killen Jr.

CSS Publishing Company, Inc.
Lima, Ohio

GOD'S NEW POSSIBILITY

Published by CSS Publishing Company, Inc., Lima, Ohio 45807. All rights re-
served. No part of this publication may be reproduced in any manner whatsoever
without the prior permission of the publisher, except in the case of brief quotations embodied in critical articles and reviews. Inquiries should be addressed to:
CSS Publishing Company, Inc., Permissions Department, 5450 N. Dixie High-
way, Lima, Ohio 45807.

Scripture quotations are from the New Revised Standard Version of the Bible.
Copyright 1989 by the Division of Christian Education of the National Council
of the Churches of Christ in the USA. Used by permission.

Library of Congress Cataloging-in-Publication Data

Killen, James L.
    God's New Possibility : Advent, Christmas, Epiphany, Cycle A / James L. Kil-
len, Jr. -- FIRST EDITION.
        pages cm
    ISBN 0-7880-2708-5 (alk. paper)
    1. Bible. N.T. Gospels--Sermons. 2. Sermons, American--21st century. 3. Advent
sermons. 4. Christmas sermons. 5. Epiphany season--Sermons. 6. Church year
sermons. 7. Common lectionary (1992). Year A. I. Title.

BS2555.54.K55 2013
252'.61--dc23

                                                  2012046838

For more information about CSS Publishing Company resources, visit our web-
site at www.csspub.com, email us at csr@csspub.com, or call (800) 241-4056.

ISBN-13: 978-0-7880-2708-6
ISBN-10: 0-7880-2708-5   PRINTED IN USA

*To Juanita
and to all who have loved me.*

Other Books by James Killen

I Believe: Daily Discoveries in the Christian Faith

Who Do You Say That I Am?: Reflections on Jesus

What Does the Lord Require?:
Meditations on Major Moral and Social Issues

Pastoral Care in Small Membership Churches

Refinery: a novel

What Can We Believe?

Table of Contents

Introduction

There are many people who wish for more from their lives than they have yet experienced. There are many who look around at all of the conflict, oppression, and suffering in the world and wish that things could be different. Some of those people come to church hoping that something will happen that can make a difference. In response to those people, God sent one who brings a new possibility, a possibility that can make things different and better in our lives and in our world. The one whom God sent came a long time ago. But the new possibility that he brought is for right here and right now.

Jesus came preaching "Repent, for the kingdom of heaven has come near" (Matthew 4:17). That was his way of announcing God's new possibility. It is the main theme of the preaching and teaching of Jesus in the gospels according to Matthew, Mark, and Luke. The gospel lessons for Advent, Christmas, and Epiphany of Cycle A in the lectionary offer exciting opportunities to discover the shape of that new possibility and the saving works of God that makes it a real possibility.

Four recurrent themes emerge from these passages that put us in touch with God's new possibility. The first is that God is real and alive and in our world right now to do the work of the Savior. We meet God and interact with God in our real life and history. The second is that God has made God's self known through the life and work of Jesus Christ and through the church's witnesses to their experience of God's saving works. The third is that if we will learn to recognize the saving work that God is doing in our lives and in our world and to respond to it, we can enter into life-shaping interactions with God and God's new possibility will become a present reality. A fourth theme is that the shape of that new possibility to which God works to save us is the life of love, a love that is a joyful commitment of life to life, a love like God's love. We hope to weave these themes together in ways that will relate meaningfully to the things that are going on in the lives of real people today.

Thank you to CSS Publishing Company for offering me the opportunity to share these messages. Thank you to my wife, Juanita, who not only proofread my manuscript but also made several significant contributions to the content of these sermons.

I also want to thank all of the congregations I have ever served and Perkins School of Theology at Southern Methodist University for being the contexts within which I have come to my understanding of the message of salvation. I especially appreciate the time I was able to spend at Perkins as a Bridwell Scholar in Residence because it was during that time that the understandings I have shared in this book approached maturity.

James L. Killen Jr.

Beyond Judgment Day

But about that day and hour no one knows, neither the angels of heaven, nor the Son, but only the Father. For as the days of Noah were, so will be the coming of the Son of Man. For as in those days before the flood they were eating and drinking, marrying and giving in marriage, until the day Noah entered the ark, and they knew nothing until the flood came and swept them all away, so too will be the coming of the Son of Man. Then two will be in the field; one will be taken and one will be left. Two women will be grinding meal together; one will be taken and one will be left. Keep awake therefore, for you do not know on what day your Lord is coming. But understand this: if the owner of the house had known in what part of the night the thief was coming, he would have stayed awake and would not have let his house be broken into. Therefore you also must be ready, for the Son of Man is coming at an unexpected hour.

One day in 1957 Dr. Albert C. Outler, a prominent theologian who was not at all prone to sensationalism, returned from a White House-sponsored conference of theologians and scientists and announced to an assembly of students at his seminary that the industrial civilization as they knew it had only a few more years to live. The subject of the conference had been the nuclear arms race. The participants were informed that the United States and the Soviet Union had both built up huge arsenals of nuclear weapons. Missiles with explosive cargos many times more destructive than those dropped on Japan were already poised and aimed at every major population center in the western world. Any act of aggression, either intentional or accidental, would provoke immediate retaliation from the enemy. It would all be over in a few hours. Dr. Outler, who was a competent historian as well as a theologian, said that in the history of the world there had never been such a buildup of arms that did not finally lead to a war. For that reason, he said he believed that there would be a terribly destructive war and that it would happen soon.

Needless to say, the announcement got the attention of the students. They began to imagine what it would be like for all of the things they thought were so substantial to be vaporized in a nuclear blast. They imagined the impressive buildings in which they met, with their massive Grecian columns, simply disappearing, and with them the shelves of books that represented the accumulated wisdom of the ages — yes, and the chapel with its hallowed traditions. Inevitably, they had to think about what it would be like for the students themselves, with all of their plans and ambitions and relationships, to simply disappear. Then, they began to wonder if the missiles were already on the way. Were there only hours or minutes left? It was a very real experience for many people in those days.

Many of the people who lived in the days during which the New Testament was written lived with a similar kind of anxiety. They believed that the world was moving toward some catastrophic end. This expectation may have been formed partially by the memory of the devastation that their people had experienced in their past at the hands of the conquering armies of the Assyrian and Babylonian empires. They knew that a similar thing could be suffered at the hands of their Roman oppressors. But the expectation had moved beyond a memory of history. It had taken a theological shape. The people believed that human history was moving toward some day of judgment that would be an act of God.

It is apparent that Jesus himself thought in those terms. The passage of scripture that we read today comes from a two-chapter collection of teachings of Jesus having to do with the last things as the people he knew expected them. In our text and several others in these two chapters, Jesus urges his followers — Jesus urges us — to keep things in perspective and to be watchful and ready for the ultimate reckoning with God.

Now, what are we to make of that? These passages have been troublesome for many people who have taken the teachings of Jesus seriously. Jesus did not come as a prophet of doom. He came as one who brings good news. Yes, he pointed forward to the coming of a new age, but it was an age of promise. The summary of his message was "repent, for the kingdom of heaven has come near" (Matthew 4:17). It is clear that when Jesus talks about the kingdom of heaven, he is not talking only about something that is to happen in the future. He is talking about a new possibility here for us in each present moment of our lives.

His teachings — the Sermon on the Mount, the parables, and all — are descriptions of the new and radically different kind of life that God makes possible for us. The two chapters in which Jesus says so much about the last days end with the familiar parable of the last judgment in which the Son of Man comes to judge all people and to separate those who are saved from those who are lost as a shepherd separates the sheep from the goats. You remember the norm by which the judgment was said to be made: "Truly I tell you, just as you did it to one of the least of these who are members of my family, you did it to me" (Matthew 25:40). It is clear that this teaching about the last days was intended to show us how to live in the here and now. In fact, that is a good way to read all of the biblical teachings about the last days. They are meant to help us get things into perspective. And the norm by which we should expect everything to be judged is the question of whether or not we have learned to live in love.

Then what is to be gained by all the talk about destruction? It helps us to put things into perspective and to distinguish between the things that are really substantial and the

11

things that are not. We have a way of getting that all mixed up and it can get in our way. Our culture keeps telling us that the really important and substantial things are things like cars, houses, office buildings, bank accounts, battleships, and missiles. We find ourselves believing that, and that belief gets in the way of our seeing life like Jesus wants us to see it. In fact, in Matthew's gospel, the thing that provoked Jesus to deliver his collection of teachings about the last days was the disciples being impressed by the structures of the temple that had been built by the old tyrant Herod the Great. Jesus said, "These buildings are just temporary. They will all eventually be torn down." And about seventy years later, during the Roman war, they were.

The students who heard Dr. Outler's attention-getting announcement found that the thoughts they had following the experience put many things into perspective. They were forced to reckon with the fact that some things they were accustomed to taking for granted were not really substantial. Fortunately, they came to learn about God, the eternal reality who gives being to all of the little temporary realities that crowd around us. The promise of God was shown to be much more substantial than the promise of a military-industrial complex. It began to make sense to organize their understanding of things around the promise of God and to let it shape their lives.

There are other ways in which life can help us get things into perspective. When a divorce, a business failure, or a major disillusionment makes life seem to fall apart, we may be pushed to take another look at the way in which we have put things together. That can be a judgment day. Ironically, a success may do the same thing. When you finally achieve all of the goals you set for yourself and have gotten all of the things you thought would make life good and discover that those goals didn't deliver what they promised, that too can be a judgment day. That can send us looking for something more substantially significant to hang our hopes on.

It is significant that Jesus talked about judgment day so that we will look for another source of hope and take hold of the promise of God. When we talk about the new age that Jesus called the kingdom of heaven, we are talking about something God has promised. That adds a new dimension to our thinking. It would be easy for us to think of it as something God requires of us. And that might seem like an overwhelming requirement. But Jesus is talking about the saving work God is doing in our lives and in our world and urging us to hang our hopes on that promise and to live toward its fulfillment.

When we talk about the saving work of God, some people may begin to visualize a promise of conspicuous miracles that will give every story a happy ending. It doesn't work like that. God is at work among all of the varied good and bad things that are going on in our lives and in history. God is at work moving things toward the fulfillment of God's good purpose for us. We are called to believe that God is at work and to look for the evidence of God's work and to try to become participants in what God is doing.

Now, what are we talking about? What does the saving work of God look like when it happens? Let's go back to our first example. More than half a century after Dr. Outler made his dire but realistic prediction, there has still not been a nuclear holocaust. The prevention of nuclear war didn't happen because God tore open the heavens and descended to destroy the nuclear arsenals. It happened through the complex interactions of the currents of history. Somehow, sanity and humanity finally prevailed. If we read the Hebrew Scriptures, we will find that is the way God worked to save the people of Israel time after time. It is interesting that one of the Old Testament prophecies of the coming day of the Lord ends with the promise "...they shall beat their swords into plowshares, and their spears into pruning hooks; nation shall not lift up sword against nation, neither shall they learn war any more" (Isaiah 2:4). What would it mean for us to believe that promise and hang our hopes upon it? The prophet invites us to come and walk in the light of the Lord.

It is a significant coincidence that the Christian season of Advent, the season of hope, comes right after the American celebration of Thanksgiving. In the Hebrew Scriptures, the hope that God will be at work in our lives and in our world to save us is rooted in the recollection of the saving works God has done in the past. Thanksgiving makes possible expectancy. How many saving works can you remember that God has done in your life? Think hard. Don't just try to remember something spectacular. Start with the recollection that God gives you life day by day. Add to that the memory that at sometime in your life, someone has loved you. Go on from there. How many things can you remember that God has done to save our nation and our world? Shake off your cultivated cynicism and look at all of the good things in our world. Remember, be thankful, and take hold of the promise that God is indeed working to bring into being a new era organized around the reality of the love of God — an era in which it will make sense to live according to the teachings of the Sermon on the Mount.

The Apostle Paul also taught us to live in the light of God's new possibility. He wrote: "…you know what time it is, how it is now the moment for you to wake from sleep. For salvation is nearer to us now than when we first became believers; the night is far gone, the day is near. Let us then lay aside the works of darkness and put on the armor of light…. put on the Lord Jesus Christ, and make no provision for the flesh, to gratify its desires" (Romans 13:11-14).

Claiming Hope

In those days John the Baptist appeared in the wilderness of Judea, proclaiming, "Repent, for the kingdom of heaven has come near." This is the one of whom the prophet Isaiah spoke when he said, "The voice of one crying out in the wilderness: 'Prepare the way of the Lord, make his paths straight.' " Now John wore clothing of camel's hair with a leather belt around his waist, and his food was locusts and wild honey. Then the people of Jerusalem and all Judea were going out to him, and all the region along the Jordan, and they were baptized by him in the river Jordan, confessing their sins. But when he saw many Pharisees and Sadducees coming for baptism, he said to them, "You brood of vipers! Who warned you to flee from the wrath to come? Bear fruit worthy of repentance. Do not presume to say to yourselves, 'We have Abraham as our ancestor'; for I tell you, God is able from these stones to raise up children to Abraham. Even now the ax is lying at the root of the trees; every tree therefore that does not bear good fruit is cut down and thrown into the fire. I baptize you with water for repentance, but one who is more powerful than I is coming after me; I am not worthy to carry his sandals. He will baptize you with the Holy Spirit and fire. His winnowing fork is in his hand, and he will clear his threshing floor and will gather his wheat into the granary; but the chaff he will burn with unquenchable fire."

"Hope" is one of the most beautiful words in the English language. It evokes thoughts of sunrises that push back all kinds of darkness. It suggests birth and healing and promise and possibility. Hope makes us able to keep on going, or if we have fallen to get up and try again. Hope is a gift that our faith can give to us that will indeed meet the need of our hungry hearts. Hope is the essence of the Christian faith. The good news is that hope is there for us. But most of us have yet to learn to discover it and take hold of it. It may be that our scripture lesson for today can help us in that regard.

Our gospel reading for today tells the first part of the story of John the Baptist. John the Baptist was a popular preacher in his day. The text says people flocked to hear him and to be baptized by him. They came from Jerusalem and Judea and from the regions around the Jordan River.

That is really kind of surprising. The picture that the text gives of him does not suggest someone who would be a popular preacher. He was dressed like the greatest maverick in Israel's history, the prophet Elijah. He laced his message with large amounts of judgment and talk about what was wrong with the world. He even got on the case of Pilate, the governor — not a very smart thing to do. He talked to people about their sins. The ritual he called people to go through was a version of the purification ritual used to bring Gentiles into the Jewish faith. You wouldn't think that would be very popular with people whose main source of self-esteem was being Jewish. Besides that, the road from Jerusalem to the Jordan River at Jericho was steep, rough, and dangerous. Yet people flocked to hear him. Why did they come?

They must have come because, when all things are considered, John preached a message of hope. His message was essentially the same as the one Jesus would soon be preaching: "Repent, the kingdom of heaven has come near."

Those were restless days in the history of Israel. The Roman army occupation could be harsh. The members of the patriot's movement, the Zealots, were always trying to stir up a revolution. The people had seen major highways lined with hundreds of bodies of rebels hung from crosses. It is hard to feel safe in that kind of an environment. Their own people were trying as best they could to cope with their situation. The Sadducees, the conservative party that held power in Jerusalem, were trying to keep peace with the Romans.

The Pharisees were trying to find stability in their religious faith, but they were going to such extremes with it that the demands they made upon the people were oppressive. The Essenes, the monastic group, were trying to withdraw from Jewish society into desert enclaves where they lived by an order so radical that they thought it would be a sin to go to the bathroom on the Sabbath. Certainly many people were restless and eager to discover a new possibility.

John came promising a new possibility. His preaching revived the people's long-cherished hope for the coming of the promised messiah.

What about us? Would we have gone out to hear John preaching his message of hope? Are we hungry for hope?

Frankly, some of us probably are not. Either we feel that we have all we want or we have some plan working that we think will meet our deepest needs as soon as we work it. Or maybe we have given up on any hope that anything can be much different from the way things are. Or maybe we just haven't thought about it.

There are times in our lives when we may feel a desperate need to recover hope. That may happen when a dream has died or we realize that something we really wanted is never going to happen. It may happen when someone has disappointed us or when we have disappointed ourselves. It may happen when our world seems to be falling apart. When the economy is failing or when everything seems to be shallow. When the political processes that we have trusted seem to be failing, or when the world seems to be full of violence and bent on self-destruction. In certain situations, we become aware of our need to recover hope. There are some of us who feel a deep need for some belief that things can be better, for ourselves, for those whom we love, and for our world.

The truth is that we need hope in our lives just as we need self-esteem, the ability to trust, or a belief that the sun will come up each morning. It is part of what makes life work. We need hope to give us a sense of expectancy that will make us want to get up in the morning and draw us forward into the living of life.

John tells us where to look for hope. Look to our belief that there is a God who loves us and to the belief that God is at work in our lives and in our world. It is strange that many of us may believe in God but do not let that belief shape our lives.

John reminded the people who came to hear him that Israel had always believed in a God who is at work to save. Their very understanding of who they were as a people was based on the memory that God had saved them from slavery in Egypt, and God had been there to reach out and save them again and again in all of the crisis times of their history. Their prophets had told them that the God who had saved them in the past would be there to save them in the future. Trusting that, the prophets promised the people that God would eventually send one who would be the savior of their nation. John reminded them of that promise. John urged them to take hold of that promise and to let it revive hope in them.

Our Christian faith gives us a similar affirmation. Jürgen Moltman, a theologian who has been teaching a theology of hope for half a century, wrote:

> …for Christians hope is the power of resurrection from life's failures and defeats. It is the power of life's rebirth out of the shadow of death. It is the power for the new beginning at the point where guilt has made life impossible. The Christian hope is all of these things because it is spirit from the Spirit of the resurrection of the betrayed, maltreated, and forsaken Christ. Through his divine raising from the dead, his hope-less end became his new beginning. If we remember that, we shall not give ourselves up, but shall expect that in every end a new beginning lies hidden.
> (*In the End — The Beginning: The Life of Hope* [Minneapolis: Fortress Press, 2004])

The hope is there for us. We just need to take hold of it. We just need to claim it. It begins by remembering what we believe about God, then reminding ourselves that God comes to meet us in every new moment of life and that God is at work in our lives and in our world to save.

It would be a mistake to be too specific about our expectations. Some people make a list of things they hope for in life, much like a child making a list of things she wants for Christmas. Then these people assume that, by prayer, they can mobilize God to make this list happen. It is much better to approach life as the apostle Paul did, confident that "all things work together for good for those who love God, who are called according to his purpose" (Romans 8:28). We should all approach life in expectancy and openness, eager to see what God will do in our lives.

John warned the people who came to hear him that there are some right ways and some wrong ways to go to meet God's new possibility. The new possibility should be allowed to change our lives. John called the people to repent, that is, to be ready to change. When John suspected that some of the religious people were just going through the motions of claiming the hope, he scolded them and told them that they must bear fruit that will show they had repented. Their lives should show it. Learn all you can about the saving work God does in people's lives. Learn all you can about the shape of the new possibility God wants for us. Then be ready to enter into a life-shaping interaction with the God who comes to meet you in life. Open yourself to his love and take it in. Let hope bring you to life.

What does it mean to take hold of hope? What does that look like? Let me tell you a story. This is a fictional story made up of a composite of the experiences of some real people.

Bill was a middle-aged man with a wife and two teenage children and a job that he liked. He was a concerned person so he was active in his church and his political party in the hope of helping to make the world a better place. Life was good for Bill and he knew it. He had the grace to be grateful that so many fortunate people lack. Bill was a person of faith and he was able to see that God was giving him life as a good gift day by day. It was fairly easy for Bill to take hold of hope and meet life expectantly.

Then things changed. There was a routine medical examination with a surprising discovery, a biopsy, and an announcement: "Bill, you have cancer, one of the bad kinds, and you need to get it attended to right away." Suddenly Bill had more things to cope with than he was able to name. There was fear, anxiety for himself and for his family, and anger. Bill was wise enough to recognize those things and deal with them. It was no longer easy to take hold of hope. But Bill knew that God works to heal, both through the scientists and medical people and also through the capacity for healing that was at work in his body. Bill made an intentional decision to take hold of hope and to let hope, rather than the other things he was feeling, guide his life.

This time, there would be a cost to claiming hope. He would have to work with the healing processes. There would be physical pain, possible disfigurement, major financial costs, and enormous inconvenience. Lots of things would have to be reorganized in Bill's life. Hope was no longer easy for Bill. He began to make some practical reorganizations of his life in case he did not survive. He began to value things differently. He began to spend more quality time with his family. When he saw a bright blue sky, he paused to enjoy it. His hope began to focus more on the present than on the future. He did what needed to be done, because he chose hope.

In spite of all efforts to defeat the disease, the doctor eventually said, "Bill, we can't cure you. You have only about a year to live." Again, Bill felt himself being drawn toward the depths of anger, despair, and hopelessness. Bill was human. He spent some time dealing with those bitter experiences. Eventually, he again chose to take hold of hope. He did a lot of talking to himself. Bill instinctively hoped that something would happen to change things, but he knew better than to count on that. He began to intentionally make the most of each day. He began to make the practical preparations for the end of his life.

Drawing on his faith, he told himself that God would still be at work in the life of his family and that others would be able to do the important things he hoped to do for them. He told himself that God would still be at work in the world, and that since he believed the things he hoped to accomplish through his religious and political endeavors were right, they would eventually prevail.

He also told himself that the God who had given him life for years is eternal and will be there to give life beyond death. In these ways Bill took hold of hope and let it shape his life. He had never been a person who thought of his faith primarily as having to do with what would come after death, but now it was time to think about that. Bill began to gather up the aspects of his tradition that had to do with that and let them minister to him. He remembered passages from scripture: "Do not let your hearts be troubled... In my Father's house there are many dwelling places" (John 14:1-2). Nothing in the whole creation, not even death, "... will be able to separate us from the love of God in Christ Jesus our Lord" (Romans 8:39). He began to remember those old songs that he used to think they sang too often: "Going home," "I'll fly away," "Tis grace that brought me safe thus far and grace will see me home," "Sing with all the saints in glory." Bill knew better than to take the words of those old songs literally, but he knew they came out of a witness of hope. He let them minister to him. He prepared to entrust himself to a hope that would take him beyond all that he had ever known.

This is a story about how one person might take hold of hope. Other stories could be told of how people coping with guilt, divorce, business failure, or many other life situations might take hold of hope. It sometimes has to be done very intentionally. It sometimes has to be a matter of choosing hope in spite of many things that would discourage. But it is the thing to do.

How might you go about taking hold of hope?

Jürgen Moltman said: "We will only become capable of new beginnings when we are prepared to let go of the things that torment us, and the things we lack. If we search for the new beginning, it will find us" (*In the End — The Beginning*).

Advent 3
Matthew 11:2-11

If You Are Looking for a Savior...

When John heard in prison what the Messiah was doing, he sent word by his disciples and said to him, "Are you the one who is to come, or are we to wait for another?" Jesus answered them, "Go and tell John what you hear and see: the blind receive their sight, the lame walk, the lepers are cleansed, the deaf hear, the dead are raised, and the poor have good news brought to them. And blessed is anyone who takes no offense at me." As they went away, Jesus began to speak to the crowds about John: "What did you go out into the wilderness to look at? A reed shaken by the wind? What then did you go out to see? Someone dressed in soft robes? Look, those who wear soft robes are in royal palaces. What then did you go out to see? A prophet? Yes, I tell you, and more than a prophet. This is the one about whom it is written, 'See, I am sending my messenger ahead of you, who will prepare your way before you.' Truly I tell you, among those born of women no one has arisen greater than John the Baptist; yet the least in the kingdom of heaven is greater than he."

If you are looking for a Savior, look where salvation is happening. That seems to be the message of today's gospel lesson. But I suppose that is not very relevant unless you believe that salvation is something that is still going on and unless you want it to happen for you.

There is some history behind this text that does not appear on the surface. John the Baptist was a popular preacher. Many people were drawn to him and he became the leader of a movement. He had followers, just as Jesus eventually did. John knew that he was not the Savior for whom the Jewish people had been waiting. John wanted God's salvation more than anything else, salvation perhaps for himself but certainly for his people and for the world. He organized his whole life around the hope for the coming of the Savior.

John believed that Jesus was the messiah. He said so when Jesus came to him to be baptized. But he and his followers did not immediately become followers of Jesus. It took Jesus a while to actually begin his ministry. There was a time of trial in the wilderness while Jesus prayed his way through to an understanding of his mission. Then Jesus returned to Galilee to begin his ministry. Jesus did not announce that he was the messiah. In fact he avoided talking about that, probably because he was afraid the people who were hoping for a military messiah would misunderstand and start a violent movement. As a result, for a while the followers of John and the followers of Jesus were two separate groups.

We can imagine that as John carried on his ministry of preaching in the southern part of the Jewish nation, he listened with great anticipation to the news of the things Jesus was doing up north in Galilee. Then John got into trouble with the governor, Herod, and was thrown into prison. He must have known that his life was in danger. Then he was even more eager to know if, in fact, the messiah for whom he was hoping had indeed come. He sent some of his followers to ask Jesus if he was the one who was to come.

Jesus did not answer directly. Instead he said,

> Go and tell John what you hear and see: the blind receive their sight, the lame walk, the lepers are cleansed, the deaf hear, the dead are raised, and the poor have good news preached to them. And blessed is anyone who takes no offense at me.
> (vv. 4-5)

These were things that the prophet Isaiah had said would happen when the messiah came to bring in God's new possibility. Jesus knew that John would understand (Isaiah 26:19; 29:18-19; 35:5-6; 42:7; 61:1).

Should we be looking for a Savior? And if so, where should we be looking?

We need to consider that question. Some of us answer too quickly. We have the idea that being saved simply means we will go to heaven when we die. Some have offered a simple answer to that: "Just believe that Jesus died to take away your guilt and you can know that you will go to heaven when you die." That is indeed part of the answer, but the Bible tells us that there is a great deal more to salvation than that.

The Hebrew Scriptures say very little about going to heaven, but they say a great deal about salvation. They present God as one who works in this life and in the history of this world to save God's people from the danger and distress of this life to a new and better possibility here and now. For them, salvation was something that was always going on.

In the New Testament, the words that are usually translated "to be saved" actually come close to meaning "to be healed" or "to be made whole." We notice that most of the signs that salvation was happening to which Isaiah and Jesus referred had to do with healing. And these different kinds of physical healing can represent several different kinds of spiritual healing. To be made able to see or to hear can mean to be made able to understand the real shape of reality and to understand the meaning of life. To be made able to walk can mean to be empowered to stand up and move out to live life fully. For a leper to be cleansed can mean to have those things taken away that cause a person to be alienated from the community and to be accepted into human relationships. For the dead to be raised can mean for those who are spiritually dead to be made able to become fully alive.

All of these things can be ways of talking about being made truly whole, to have the kind of life that God wants us to have. Throughout the Bible, the saving work of God had to do with God saving us from those things that cripple our humanity, things like greed and fear and hate as well as from external oppression. It has to do with God saving us to a new kind of life, life in which the image of God is renewed in us. The simplest explanation of the life that God wants to save us to is to say that God wants us to learn to love. God wants us to learn to love as God loves. That is the objective of God's saving work.

When Jesus said that "the poor have good news brought to them," he was talking about another dimension of God's saving work, the renewal of human society as a whole so that a new age of justice for all people would be ushered in. That too is a matter of enabling all humankind to live in love. All of these things are parts of what the Bible means when it talks about salvation.

All of that adds new dimensions to the question about looking for a savior, doesn't it? Well, how about it? Do we want to go looking for a savior? You probably hadn't thought of that lately, had you?

We don't have to spend much time watching the evening news on television to see that lots of things are going wrong in our world. There is so much violence, corruption, and human suffering. Lots of people and movements seem to be offering themselves as saviors. But most of them don't seem to be making salvation happen.

When we look within ourselves, do we find real wholeness? Are there any things that you need to be saved from, things that may be crippling your humanity and keeping you from living life as fully as you could? I suppose the best question to ask is: Are you able to love? Are you able to love yourself, not with a greedy selfishness, but with a joyful, healthy self-affirmation that allows you to say "yes" to yourself and "yes" to life and to live fully and freely? Are you able to love life?

Think seriously about that. Are you really able to love life as you have it now and get excited about life as it can be? Are you able to love others with the same kind of love you have for yourself or could have? Are you really happy with even the love you share with those who are closest to you? And how wide is that circle within which you love? God wants us to love everybody. Yes, everybody. That is what will make real fullness of life possible for us and will finally make survival possible for humanity as a whole. Now those of you who hang around the church house are probably expecting me to ask if you love God. Yes, that is part of it. But if you love in all of those other ways, you will be loving God.

How about it? Could we interest you in some salvation? Do you need a savior? Don't answer right now. Just think about it.

The people of Israel had the teachings of the prophets to help them recognize when salvation is happening. We have something better than that. We have the memory of Jesus. God sent Jesus to make God known. He lived among us but he did the saving works of God. Yes, works. Jesus found people and communities in all sorts of different conditions of need and of possibility and he related himself to them in ways that were appropriate to their different needs. He healed some. He brought some under judgment so they realized that they needed to make some changes. He forgave some who were crippled by guilt. He liberated some who were oppressed, either by something within them or by something without. And when he found some who were strong, he called them to reorganize their lives around a new purpose and to become servants of God. There were some whom he just loved into life. The knowledge that God loves us enough to reach out to us in costly commitment was enough to make the big difference in their lives. All of those were saving works of God. And there were others. The people who wrote the Bible told stories of how God worked through Jesus to save them to fullness of life. We can read the story of Jesus and learn how God saves.

Here is something interesting. Many of the names by which Jesus was called in the Bible actually represent stories that some of the early Christians told to witness to the saving works of God that they experienced through interactions with Jesus. The stories were different because Jesus found people in different situations of need and related to each of them in ways that were appropriate to their situations. Those who called him the Word experienced him as one who told them the secret of the meaning of life. Those who called him Son of Man experienced him as one who had shown them the need for change and called them to repentance. Those who called him Messiah experienced him as the one who brings a new possibility.

And here is the key. God is still at work in our lives and in our world to do the same kinds of saving works that God did through Jesus. When we see those things happening, either in our lives or in our world, we will know that the Savior is at work there. We can open ourselves to that saving work and let it happen to us and through us.

Then where should we look to find the saving works of God happening? Some think it can happen only in some spectacular event when some awesome being crashes through the skies, does something that violates six of the laws of nature, and then disappears in a postlude of ethereal music. That doesn't happen very often. If we know how to recognize what God is doing, we can find him at work to save in many of the down-to-earth happenings of our lives.

For example, have you ever come to a time in your life when you realized that things just were not working? Perhaps there was something wrong with the way in which you put life together. That realization may break in upon you in the midst of angry frustration. But it can force you to come to grips with the fact that some changes must be made. It can be helpful in that situation to remember that Jesus sometimes confronted people with a need to change. Jesus came preaching the same message that John preached: "The time is fulfilled, and the kingdom of God has come near; repent, and believe the good news" (Mark 1:15). There is that word "repent." It means get ready to make some changes. And for Jesus, it was a part of the good news that God was opening a new possibility for humankind. That recollection may make you wonder if some new and better possibility is being made available to you. Could this unhappy situation actually be one of the saving works of God? It is worth asking the question.

Or imagine a happier situation, one in which you enjoy being in the circle of a loving family or a circle of good friends. In that set of relationships, you feel yourself being accepted as you are, valued as a person, and loved. In that kind of situation you can experience forgiveness, healing, and enablement. You can experience your own personhood emerging. That is definitely a saving work of God, the work that church people call grace. We can remember Jesus did that sort of thing for people whom he met during his ministry, and we can recognize it as a saving work of God.

If you are worried about all of the bad things that are going on in the world, look for some of the movements that are making things better and bringing hope. Yes, there are some. God may be calling you to become a participant in some of those movements. That commitment will give new meaning to your life. Can you remember Jesus calling people to follow him and become his disciples? That too is a saving work.

If you are looking for a Savior — and we all need to be looking for a Savior — look for the places where salvation is happening. Go there. Open yourself to it. Let it happen in you and through you.

Look Again

Now the birth of Jesus the Messiah took place in this way. When his mother Mary had been engaged to Joseph, but before they lived together, she was found to be with child from the Holy Spirit. Her husband Joseph, being a righteous man and unwilling to expose her to public disgrace, planned to dismiss her quietly. But just when he had resolved to do this, an angel of the Lord appeared to him in a dream and said, "Joseph, son of David, do not be afraid to take Mary as your wife, for the child conceived in her is from the Holy Spirit. She will bear a son, and you are to name him Jesus, for he will save his people from their sins." All this took place to fulfill what had been spoken by the Lord through the prophet: "Look, the virgin shall conceive and bear a son, and they shall name him Emmanuel," which means, "God is with us." When Joseph awoke from sleep, he did as the angel of the Lord commanded him; he took her as his wife, but had no marital relations with her until she had borne a son; and he named him Jesus.

When you look out at the world you live in, what do you see? At first, many of us tend to see things that are disturbing and threatening. That may not be all there is out there, but those are the things we tend to see first. The newspapers are full of terrible news. There are reports of oppression and violence in other countries and of international tensions that threaten our own sense of security. We hear about terrorism and the threat of terrorism. We are reminded that the threat of destruction by nuclear weapons has not entirely disappeared from the world.

We read reports of economic instability that make us anxious about keeping the level of prosperity that we have.

We hear of corruption and abuses of power in business and government that make us lose confidence in some of the structures of community we need to be able to trust. Around us we see evidence of erosion of moral standards that seem to threaten our value systems.

Some of us can look closer to home and see other things that are disturbing to us, conflicts between family members, anxieties about our children or our parents, anxieties about whether we can stay employed or make ends meet with our income. Some of us even look within ourselves and see things that make us feel not okay.

Knowing that we have to live in that world can cause lots of anxieties. We may even feel like we want to run and hide.

Lots of people must have had similar feelings in the days when the biblical drama was being played out. There were tensions between the religious and ethnic groups within the Jewish nation. The poor were very poor and struggled to survive, and the whole country lived under the oppression of an anxious tyrant who was so cruel that he had several members of his own family killed because he imagined they were threats to his power.

In addition to these things, a certain young carpenter named Joseph had some other things to worry about. He was engaged to a young woman named Mary. He was looking forward to all of the things that young engaged people look forward to. But he just learned that his fiancée was pregnant and he knew he was not the father. He felt a lot of hurt and anger. He knew that Jewish law allowed him to have her stoned to death but he didn't want to do that. He didn't know what he should do. He was ready to terminate the engagement quietly and try as best he could to put his life together again.

Then Joseph had a dream. An angel came to him and told him not to be afraid to take Mary as his wife because her pregnancy was an act of God. She was chosen to be the mother of the long-expected messiah. And Joseph would have an important role to play in the working out of the purpose of God. The angel spoke of two names by which the child might be called. He would be the fulfillment of a prophecy of Isaiah of a messiah who would be called "Emmanuel," which means "God with us" or "God is with us." But the angel told Joseph that he was to name the child "Jesus," which means "God's salvation."

When Joseph woke up, he must have thought a lot about the dream. Finally he decided to take it seriously. He believed God was about to do saving work in the world and that he would have a role to play in it. He had no idea what would be required of him, but he was willing to do whatever was necessary to participate in the saving work of God.

After the dream, life must have looked very different to Joseph. He saw his own situation in a different light. He was no longer a betrayed fiancé. He was a man chosen to do something special and demanding in the service of God. And the world looked different to him too. King Herod was still a force to be reckoned with. But now he knew that someone greater than Herod was at work in the world. God was active with the people. All of the problems of God's people were made subject to a new possibility that was breaking in upon the world, because someone was coming who would be God's salvation.

Joseph must have played an important role in the life of Jesus as he was growing up. He did not live long enough to see Jesus carry on his ministry in the world. But others did. They saw how Jesus represented God present with us. He made God known. He showed us the many ways in which God works to save, and those things Jesus showed us about God are still true.

What can it mean to know that God is with us in this world and in this life? We are far too accustomed to thinking that God is far away — somewhere beyond the sky — and that God is absent when some of the important things of our lives are happening. What would it mean to be able to believe we live in a God-invaded world, a world in which God is present with us? What could it mean to believe that God is at work in our world doing things that will move us and our world toward salvation?

We started by talking about how this world we live in usually looks to us. If we believe those things Jesus has taught us to believe about God, we may want to take another look. Things just may look different.

It would be a mistake for us to believe that everything happening in our world is something God decided to cause to happen. No, God has chosen to put things together in this world so that there is an openness and so that all sorts of things are possible, both good things and bad things. Many of the threatening things we spoke about when we were talking about how life looks to us are real destructive forces that have to be dealt with, just as King Herod was a real threat Joseph and Mary had to deal with. But God is at work in our world too. God is at work in all of those people and forces that tend to pull things together and make things work and move toward the fulfillment of their best possibilities. The Bible teaches us that those forces through which God is working will ultimately win the future. When we look at life in our world, it is natural for us to see first the threatening things. But we need to look again and see the promising things happening in the world and recognize that God is at work in them.

When we are overwhelmed with the problems of our lives, it is natural to see only the problems. They seem so big that they may blot out the sky. But in those times we need to look again and see the things happening in our world and in our lives that represent the saving work of God. It is important for us to study the biblical message so that we can understand what the shape of God's salvation is and be able to recognize the kinds of things that God does to save. It is much too easy for us to dream up our own ideas about what the solution to our problems and the world's problems should be and then to try to enlist God to accomplish our plans. It is important to remember how Jesus worked to save and then to watch for those happenings in our lives and in our world. When we see those things happening, we can take hope. We can open ourselves to them. We can commit ourselves to them. And like Joseph and Mary, we can become participants in God's saving work.

As we read the gospel of Matthew, we are going to see how Jesus came to bring an entirely new possibility to the world, a possibility called the kingdom of heaven. This is not just a little adornment to be added to the edge of our lives or a reward to be tacked on to the ends of our lives. It is a total reorganization of life around a new center. It is a reorganization of life in the world so that there will be new values, new ways of seeing things, new ways of doing things, and new things to be doing.

Jesus comes to us as individuals and offers us a new possibility that will reorganize our lives. This reorganization can indeed make a difference. Some of the things that seem threatening to us may have their roots in conditions in our own lives that need to be changed. New possibilities may give us reasons to look again at some of the things that are going on in our own lives. They may look different now.

Not a few people who have organized their lives around the one purpose of becoming financially affluent have come to recognize that those things that frustrated their efforts to become rich and forced them to find something better to live for were indeed saving works of God. Not a few have found a richer, better life after the reorganization. They have learned to take another look and see things differently.

Sometimes we need to look again at the happenings in

our world. When we see them in the light of God's saving work, they may look different to us. There was a time when the civil rights movement seemed the most threatening thing in the world for many people. They thought that it threatened everything they held dear. But in time most of us have come to realize that God was at work in that movement, and the reorganization of life that it has brought has saved our world from something very bad. Some people have found that, in the long run, it eventually saved them from the oppression of fear and hatred. We have learned to look again at the things that were happening.

There is a story in the second book of Kings in the Old Testament that is very interesting (2 Kings 6:8-23). The prophet Elisha provoked the anger of the king of Aram by repeatedly warning the king of Israel how to avoid the attacks of the Arameans. When the king of Aram learned it was the prophet that was his undoing and that the prophet was staying at Dothan, he sent an army to surround the city by night so they could capture Elisha in the morning. One of the servants of Elisha got up early and went out and saw that the city was surrounded. He came back and told the prophet. Elisha replied, "Do not be afraid, for there are more with us than there are with them" (v. 16). Elisha prayed for his servant and his eyes were opened and he saw that there were horses and chariots of fire all around Elisha. Then Elisha performed a miracle that prevented a war and caused the Arameans to stop coming against Israel. When we are on the Lord's side, there are always more with us than there are against us.

When we look at life and find it full of hurtful and threatening things, let's remember that God is in this world and God is at work to save. Then let's look again.

Called to Participate

In those days a decree went out from Emperor Augustus that all the world should be registered. This was the first registration and was taken while Quirinius was governor of Syria. All went to their own towns to be registered. Joseph also went from the town of Nazareth in Galilee to Judea, to the city of David called Bethlehem, because he was descended from the house and family of David. He went to be registered with Mary, to whom he was engaged and who was expecting a child. While they were there, the time came for her to deliver her child. And she gave birth to her firstborn son and wrapped him in bands of cloth, and laid him in a manger, because there was no place for them in the inn. In that region there were shepherds living in the fields, keeping watch over their flock by night. Then an angel of the Lord stood before them, and the glory of the Lord shone around them, and they were terrified. But the angel said to them, "Do not be afraid; for see — I am bringing you good news of great joy for all the people: to you is born this day in the city of David a Savior, who is the Messiah, the Lord. This will be a sign for you: you will find a child wrapped in bands of cloth and lying in a manger." And suddenly there was with the angel a multitude of the heavenly host, praising God and saying, "Glory to God in the highest heaven, and on earth peace among those whom he favors!"

How beautiful is the nativity story and how precious to us. In fact, the story has become so precious to us that we sometimes forget its importance and what it can and should mean to us. This is the story of the beginning of a saving work of God that has been pivotal in human history and in the lives of many people. God was doing something to change the course of human life and history. But God chose to do his work in ways that call for the participation of the people involved. Otherwise it would not have been real. God could have waved his hand and made everything good. But that is not the kind of goodness that God wants for us. God wants for us the kind of goodness with which God is good and that requires a choice. That requires participation. It required the participation of the people involved in the story. And it requires our participation too.

The story of the birth of Jesus actually started nine months before the night described in our reading for tonight. It started one day when a young teenage girl from a poor family, going about her daily chores, went down to the village well to draw water for her family. As people in her culture evaluated things, there could hardly have been a less significant person. On the way, she met a stranger and he spoke to her, saying: "Greetings, favored one. The Lord is with you" (Luke 1:28). Mary was bewildered by this. The stranger explained that God was about to do the saving work for which the people of Israel had been hoping for centuries. There was to be a role in that work for Mary. She was to bear the child who would be the messiah. She could hardly have imagined what all that would require of her. But she must have known it would require the commitment of her whole life. She had a decision to make. She could have dropped her water jar and run home. But instead she chose to respond in faith and in obedience to the purpose of God. She said, "Here am I, the servant of the Lord; let it be with me according to your word" (Luke 1:38). And so the story began (Luke 1:26-38).

There would be others who would make decisions to be participants in the story: a young carpenter who was engaged to Mary, the people of a little village, a group of shepherds. Down through the years many have been called to participate in the saving work of God. They all had decisions to make. And we are called to participate in the saving work of

God. We have decisions to make as well. Let's talk about the ways in which we are called to participate in the saving work of God and about the decisions we make.

We who live on this side of the nativity are able to know the whole story of the life that began in Bethlehem. We are able to know how it ended, with the one who represented God to us dying upon a cross to show us how great and unconditional God's love is for us. The meaning is there for us. Our guilt, brokenness, and unworthiness have been set aside and we have been freely given the status of beloved children of God. Some of us have grown up knowing ourselves to be beloved children of God. Others of us have to come to that discovery struggling through the turmoil of painfully neglected or broken lives. And maybe some of us have not yet come to that discovery. Some of us who have always heard that we are the beloved children of God have yet to really take in all that can mean.

This is where it must start for each of us. It starts with your willingness for God's saving work to be done in your own lives. And that begins with discovering all that it can mean to know that God loves you and has chosen you as one of God's beloved children. That may come to you in one magnificent realization or in a gradually unfolding awareness. However it comes, when you hear the news that you are a chosen child of God, you must make a decision. Will you choose to accept that as your identity and let it be who you are? Will you be able to say, "Let it be with me according to your word"?

That is only the beginning. God's saving work continues to go on in your life. Every day of your life God comes to meet you through your experiences. God is constantly interacting with you, whether you know it or not. God is working to reshape your life. What is it that God is trying to do in your life? God is trying to teach you to love. God is trying to teach you to love as God loves. Lots of us have a hard time understanding what that means. Our culture has such a distorted understanding of love that the word is almost useless. But the reality is essential. In the life of Jesus, God has shown us what real love is. In fact, in the whole biblical saga God has shown us what real love is. Love is a commitment of life to life that is freely and joyfully made. It is being committed to fullness of life for yourself, and for others, and for the whole creation. It is the willingness to do all you can to make that fullness of life possible. That is the way in which God loves. That is the way in which God wants you to love. That is not an easy thing to do. Many of us do not have it within ourselves to love in that way. We must be realistic about that. If we let love shape our lives instead of some of the things that are shaping them now, we may find ourselves living very different lives. But if we let our lives be reshaped day by day through our interactions with the God who is at work in our lives, God will love us into the ability to love. Are you willing for that to happen to you? Are you willing to say, "Let it be with me according to your word"?

But God's love is not just for us. It is for the whole world. A healthy love may begin with love for yourself, but it cannot stop there. By its very nature, real love is something that grows. It enlarges its circle and includes more and more people. And that is part of God's plan for the salvation of the world. Our world is full of hurt, lonely, and broken people who need to be loved into wholeness. Some of the people are very near to you, sitting on the same pew with you, maybe living at your house with you. Many others are within your reach. Some of them are the troublesome people you keep hoping you don't have to meet. Some of them are the people you see on the streets who seem to have trashed out their lives. Some of them may even be people you have identified as your enemies. Some are close at hand. Some live on the other side of the world. But God loves them all. God wants to love them into wholeness. God wants to work through you to reach out to those people in love. That is an important part of the way in which God does the saving work in the world. God calls you to participate in it. Are you willing to say, "Let it be with me according to your word"?

There is a special way in which God needs for us to express our love, and it seems to be much more difficult for many of us than it should be. God needs for us to speak to others about the love of God for them and about the new possibility God has for their lives. There are people within your circle of relationships who need someone to talk to them about this story we are sharing. It really is not hard to do. Just say something to those who are near to you about the faith that has become important to you and see if they want to talk about it. If they don't want to talk about it, just offer to talk about it some other time if they would like. If they do want to talk about it, just share what is real to you in the simplest and most loving way you can. It is something that really needs to happen, and God needs for you to do it. Are you willing to say, "Let it be with me according to your word"?

Not everything that God calls us to do is easy. There are things that need to be changed in our world, big things, things that are causing massive amounts of human suffering, things that could even threaten the future of the human race. Those things will not be changed unless people who are committed to justice and well-being for all will wade into the conflicted situations of human life and history and do what needs to be done to make things different. Watch the local and world news on your television and ask yourself, "What does God really want to do as a saving work in those situations?" What does love call you to do?

You may find yourself called to do something very costly and demanding. A number of years ago when violent political oppression was rampant in some Latin American countries, many refugees came north into this country to seek refuge and to save their lives. Even though they were present in this country illegally, many churches felt compelled to give the people refuge. A lay leader of one of the churches had a hard time dealing with that. He was an attorney and a former law enforcement officer. So far as he was concerned, anything that was illegal was just plain wrong. He decided to investigate. Before he had finished his investigation, he found that the historical realities of the situation challenged his deeply held belief. Eventually he felt called by God to become active in support of the cause of the refugees. God can call us to do unexpected things.

Can you handle being called by God into involvement in something that would be costly and difficult? Are you able to say, "Let it be with me according to your word"?

We have read the precious story of the beginning of God's greatest saving work. It is something that God did. God called some very ordinary people to participate in God's saving work. That is the way God does it. God is still doing saving works in the lives of people and in our world today. There are other beautiful stories to be told if we are willing to participate with God in the saving work that God is doing.

Now let us bow for a time of silent prayer. Let us think about the things that God may want to do in our lives and in our world. Let us think about what God may be calling us to do. When we are ready, if we are ready, let us silently pray the words "Let it be with me according to your word."

Weeping at Christmastime

Now after they had left, an angel of the Lord appeared to Joseph in a dream and said, "Get up, take the child and his mother, and flee to Egypt, and remain there until I tell you; for Herod is about to search for the child, to destroy him." Then Joseph got up, took the child and his mother by night, and went to Egypt, and remained there until the death of Herod. This was to fulfill what had been spoken by the Lord through the prophet, "Out of Egypt I have called my son." When Herod saw that he had been tricked by the wise men, he was infuriated, and he sent and killed all the children in and around Bethlehem who were two years old or under, according to the time that he had learned from the wise men. Then was fulfilled what had been spoken through the prophet Jeremiah: "A voice was heard in Ramah, wailing and loud lamentation, Rachel weeping for her children; she refused to be consoled, because they are no more." When Herod died, an angel of the Lord suddenly appeared in a dream to Joseph in Egypt and said, "Get up, take the child and his mother, and go to the land of Israel, for those who were seeking the child's life are dead." Then Joseph got up, took the child and his mother, and went to the land of Israel. But when he heard that Archelaus was ruling over Judea in place of his father Herod, he was afraid to go there. And after being warned in a dream, he went away to the district of Galilee. There he made his home in a town called Nazareth, so that what had been spoken through the prophets might be fulfilled, "He will be called a Nazorean."

The scripture lesson we read today is certainly not our favorite part of the Christmas story. But I suppose we really need for it to be in there. We have surrounded our Christmas traditions with such beauty and serenity that we may sometimes wonder if those traditions have anything to do with the real world in which we live. Sometimes, as we stand gazing at the baby in the center of the manger scene or tearing up during the children's Christmas pageant or as we sing "Silent Night" by candlelight at the end of a Christmas Eve service, we may begin to hear a somber voice speaking in the back of our minds. And the voice will say: Auschwitz, Nanking, Pearl Harbor, Hiroshima, Cambodia, MyLai, Rwanda, Bosnia, 9/11, Gaza. It is meaningful for us to be reminded that the story of the birth of Christ took place in a world where tyrants think nothing of massacring innocent people to retain their power — even while they are patronizing the traditions of religion, where persecuted people have to become refugees, and where nations go to war with each other and leave mothers weeping for their children because they are no more.

Every year there are those who come to Christmas with personal sadness or suffering that only becomes deeper during the season when they can remember sharing Christmas with people they loved but who are gone now. The first Christmas without a well-loved child or partner can be terribly difficult. So can a Christmas when you are thinking about the possibility that it may be your last Christmas.

Now there are lots of us who come to Christmas anxious about our family's financial well-being because a job has been lost or is in jeopardy. That makes it awfully hard to celebrate, especially in a culture that has taught us that celebrating involves spending money.

There are lots of people for whom the words of the Christmas story that ring most true are those that say: "A voice was heard in Ramah, wailing and loud lamentation, Rachel weeping for her children; she refuses to be consoled, because they are no more" (Matthew 2:18).

It is good that those words are in this story. They assure us that God understands human grief and suffering and all of the other inner and outer oppressions of our lives. God has drawn near to us as we experience those things to put loving arms around us and comfort us.

But there is more to what God did in this special event than just to pay a sympathy call. God has reached out to make life, even fullness of life, possible under our circumstances.

There are aspects of the meaning of the birth of Christ that cannot be fully understood except by looking back on the whole story that began with that birth and reflecting upon what it means to people whose lives have been impacted by it. Late in the time when the Bible was being written, the unknown Christian who wrote the book of Hebrews gathered up several of the witnesses of the people who had experienced God's saving work and wove them into a narrative that makes the story relevant to our experience of life in the real world. Let's look at some of the high points of that story and see what help they offer us.

The writer begins his book by making it clear that the main actor in this story is God, who "has spoken to us by a Son, whom he appointed heir of all things, through whom he also created the worlds," and who is "the exact imprint of God's very being" (Hebrews 1:2-3). Then the writer tells us that the one whom God had chosen to be the pioneer of our salvation came to live among us as one of us to experience everything that we experience: the trials, the suffering, and even the temptations. He came to identify with us like a member of our family, a big brother, who has come to share life with us so that he can work with us for our salvation (Hebrews 2:10-13).

When we are experiencing the suffering and the trials that are part of life in the real world, it can mean a lot to know that God loves us enough to come and join us and to share in our suffering. Many suffering people in Catholic countries have found great comfort in kissing the feet of the image of Christ hanging on a cross. It helps to know that God loves us that much.

Then the writer tells us that, having joined with us in our human situation, God does some things that make it possible for us to break loose from the bondage of our human situation and live the life for which we were created — even under our circumstances in this real world. The writer speaks of Christ making atonement for our sins so that we need no longer to be crippled by our guilt. He speaks of Jesus defeating death so that we need no longer let the fear of death rule our lives. Then the writer tells us that Jesus actually lived the life of love in obedience to the purpose of God, the life for which we were created, under circumstances like our own. He did that to set an example and to demonstrate to us that it is possible for us (Hebrews 2:14-18).

In saying these things, the writer reminds us of several of the great biblical witnesses to the saving work that God is doing in the lives of those who will be open to his saving work. God forgives our sins. That is part of what we need. We can't live in this world without participating in some ways in its wrongness — the very wrongness that causes so much human suffering. We need to know that we can be forgiven so that we can keep on living.

We need to be set free from the fear of death and of all the other threats by which the tyrannies of our world work to rule our lives. It takes great courage to claim freedom and to live in it. But God wants us to have it. The suffering in the world calls us to move out into the world and live in love and obedience to the purpose of God so that God can use us to make the world better. The God who came to live among us will not allow us to cave in to self-pity. God is a God of high expectations. But God is a God who works with us to make possible all that is required of us.

Then the writer of the book of Hebrews moves on to another phase of the story of what God does for our salvation.

He tells us that the one who came to live among us and share life with us has returned to be an aspect of the eternal reality of God. He uses several picturesque images to describe this. He pictures Jesus sitting at the right hand of the throne of God, participating with God in ruling all reality. He also pictures Jesus acting as a great high priest in a great temple in heaven, representing us before God and making sacrifices to atone for our sins. These are the kinds of classical images we can't take literally anymore. But we can try to look behind them and ask "What do they really mean?" As if to help us do that, the writer says:

> For we do not have a high priest who is unable to sympathize with our weakness, but we have one who in every respect has been tested as we are, yet without sin. Let us therefore approach the throne of grace with boldness, so that we may receive mercy and find grace to help in time of need.
> (Hebrews 4:15-16)

That says it all, doesn't it? God understands. God is there to help when the going gets rough. We can move into life with courage because we know that the one who is watching understands and there is someone to help.

If we set aside all of the complicated geography of heaven, we can remember that we are talking about a God who is alive and walking by our side and looking for ways to reach out to us. We have a God who knows about our suffering and cares deeply about it and shares in it with us. When we cry, God cries. And God comes to us in our times of trial and works with us to enable us to make the most of life under our circumstances. God is a God who expects us to take the help he gives and to do all we can to make the most of life. But God is also a God who understands when we stumble and is there to help us get up and keep on going.

When and where does God do those things? They are nice ideas but they don't help much if they are just abstractions.

We must believe that God is reaching out to do those things for us through the experiences and relationships of life. There are those in our world who cause suffering. But there are also those who embody God's saving work. Look for them. Respond to them. When we are hurting, know that the person who comes to express sincere sympathy has been sent by God. Know that the one who has suffered a similar hurt can offer you real understanding. Know that those who keep on loving you even after you have messed things up are representatives of God's forgiving grace. Those people, whom you admire because they have made the most of life in spite of harsh circumstances, may actually represent the pioneer of God's salvation to you because they show you that it is possible. Even the friend who comes to you and tells you to stop feeling sorry for yourself and to get up and get busy living may be an agent of the God of high expectations. That may seem harsh at the time, but if it is done in love it may be a representation of God. And know for certain that the friends who are beside you as you cope with the trials of life are agents of God's salvation.

Look for those whom God may be using to make life possible for you. Then look for those situations in which God may want to use you as an agent of God's saving work.

God heard Rachel weeping for her children. God heard the mothers of the babies whom Herod slaughtered crying out in anguish. God hears us when we are in grief or pain or fear. God cares because God loves us. God comes to stand by our side and make life possible even when life is at its worst.

New Year's Resolutions

When the Son of Man comes in his glory, and all the angels with him, then he will sit on the throne of his glory. All the nations will be gathered before him, and he will separate people one from another as a shepherd separates the sheep from the goats, and he will put the sheep at his right hand and the goats at the left. Then the king will say to those at his right hand, "Come, you that are blessed by my Father, inherit the kingdom prepared for you from the foundation of the world; for I was hungry and you gave me food, I was thirsty and you gave me something to drink, I was a stranger and you welcomed me, I was naked and you gave me clothing, I was sick and you took care of me, I was in prison and you visited me." Then the righteous will answer him, "Lord, when was it that we saw you hungry and gave you food, or thirsty and gave you something to drink? And when was it that we saw you a stranger and welcomed you, or naked and gave you clothing? And when was it that we saw you sick or in prison and visited you?" And the king will answer them, "Truly I tell you, just as you did it to one of the least of these who are members of my family, you did it to me." Then he will say to those at his left hand, "You that are accursed, depart from me into the eternal fire prepared for the devil and his angels; for I was hungry and you gave me no food, I was thirsty and you gave me nothing to drink, I was a stranger and you did not welcome me, naked and you did not give me clothing, sick and in prison and you did not visit me." Then they also will answer, "Lord, when was it that we saw you hungry or thirsty or a stranger or naked or sick or in prison, and did not take care of you?" Then he will answer them, "Truly I tell you, just as you did not do it to one of the least of these, you did not do it to me." And these will go away into eternal punishment, but the righteous into eternal life.

You know, there is something about New Year's Day that is a little bit like judgment day. It is a time when we look back and ask ourselves if we feel good about what we did with the year just past. Fortunately, for most of us, New Year's Day is a judgment day with the promise of another year — another possibility — a chance to do better attached. When old age or serious illness makes us wonder how many chances we have left, we may take the opportunity very seriously. We all should take it seriously. None of us know how many chances we have left to make the most of life. Assuming we all have at least one more chance, let's seek some biblical guidance to see how we can make the most of it.

There is a theme in the New Testament that comes close to reflecting the same kind of situation. Many of the Jewish people who lived during the time of Jesus believed that human history would soon come to an end. They expected that there would be a judgment day on which all people would appear before the judgment seat of God and a verdict would be pronounced on each of them. The righteous would be received into eternal bliss and the unrighteous would be condemned to eternal torment.

There was a belief among some of the Jewish people that, just before that final time of judgment, God would send an agent to warn the people of the coming crisis, show them the wrongness in their lives, and urge them to make needed changes before it was too late. Some people called that agent of warning "the prophet of the last days" and some referred to him as "the Son of Man." The beliefs about that expectation are varied and ambiguous in the Jewish literature of the time.

There is something interesting about the idea of the Son of Man. Jesus seems to understand his own mission, at least partially, in terms of doing the work of the Son of Man. He even called himself by that name. None of the Bible writers seem to have understood his mission in that way or called him by that name. But in the quotations in which Jesus spoke of himself, he most often referred to himself as the Son of Man. He evidently felt that it was his mission to confront people and communities with the things that needed fixing in their lives, to offer them a better possibility, and to call them to make needed changes. The word he used was "repent."

Now here is something important to remember. In the New Testament there is a difference between judgment and condemnation. Judgment is a loving act by someone who wants to help you avoid condemnation. It always offers a better possibility, another chance. Jesus seemed to be always calling people to make new year's resolutions.

As we look to find the risen Christ, the living God, at work to save in our lives, we may find that we often encounter him in crisis situations. He comes to us when circumstances force us to reckon with the fact that things as they are not working and we need to make some changes. We may very well encounter the Son of Man as we look back on our year just past and make resolutions about what to do differently in the coming year.

Jesus does more than just remind us that we need to make some resolutions. He is eager to give guidance about the resolutions we should make. Most of us could use some help with that. We are good at thinking up resolutions. We are going to get organized, study harder in school, or lose weight. But most of our resolutions are pretty superficial. They would not make much difference in our lives even if we actually followed through with them. Jesus has a better suggestion.

Our scripture lesson for today is the parable of the last judgment in Matthew 25:31-46. In it, Jesus describes the last judgment when the Son of Man will come in his glory and the peoples of all nations will come before him for the final judgment. Jesus says that the Son of Man will say to some:

Come, you that are blessed by my Father, inherit the kingdom prepared for you from the foundation of the world; for I was hungry and you gave me food, I was thirsty and you gave me something to drink, I was a stranger and you welcomed me, I was naked and you gave me clothing.
(vv. 34-36)

Then the blessed will ask, "When did we do those things for you?" And the king shall answer, "Truly I tell you, just as you did it to one of the least of these who are members of my family, you did it for me" (v. 40). Then do you remember what the judge said to those who did not pass that test? "You that are accursed, depart from me into the eternal fire prepared for the devil and his angels..." (v. 41).

Gulp! That can take us by surprise, especially now that many people have developed a philosophy of life that makes them feel self-righteous about their selfishness and causes them to make loud speeches announcing that if a person is hungry it is because he is too lazy to work and the only thing that is significant about an alien is that he is illegal. Some people find comfort in that way of thinking, even though it is for the most part out of touch with the realities in today's world. When we apply that standard of judgment to our families, churches, communities, and political parties we can sometimes find ourselves saying "Gulp! Gulp! Gulp!" again.

Really now, is that all that God cares about? Is it all a matter of chalking up a good record with the local charities? No, of course it is not. Those things Jesus mentioned are just outward signs that may appear on the surface as evidence of something much bigger working at a deeper level in life. And what is that? It is a life lived in love. That is what God wants from us and for us. That is the truly good life to which God wants to save us. How have we missed that? Salvation is not just a matter of having confirmed reservations in Hotel Heaven. That is a good gift from God but God wants even more from us and for us. God wants us to live in love, just as God lives in love. The Bible makes that clear.

Many of us have a problem with the idea of living in love. Even if we have managed not to slip into the popular notion that love is mostly about sex, we are likely to think of it as a matter of warm sentimental emotion. We can't see how that could equip us to cope with the tough realities of life in the real world.

If we study our Bibles, we find a much different and more substantial understanding of what love is. Let's look at the best known verse in the whole New Testament: "God so loved the world that he gave his only Son, so that everyone who believes in him may not perish but may have eternal life" (John 3:16). What does the word "love" represent in that context? It is much more than a warm emotion. In that context, the word "love" represents a commitment, a commitment of life to life, it is wanting for all who are loved what is really best. It is a willingness to give yourself, in costly ways if necessary, and enable what is best to happen. Yes, that is a much more substantial notion of what love is. That can indeed equip a person to cope with the tough realities of life.

We don't like that idea very much. It runs counter to our precious selfishness. We don't like to make commitments. In fact, many in our culture are trying hard to develop a notion of love between a man and a woman that does not involve commitment — but it doesn't work. It takes commitment to make life work.

The Bible has a lot more to say about love. If you want to do something really interesting, read the first three chapters of Genesis to see the shape of the love that God lived out in relationship to the first creatures. There you will find a love that begins with a healthy love for self. God must have loved God's self since there was no one else to love. But it was not a selfish attitude that draws in upon self, it was a dynamic self-affirmation that filled God to overflowing and caused God to reach out to others and call other realities into being so that love can be shared. When God called others into being, God gave them freedom and responsibility and respected their separateness so that they could eventually learn to love as God loves. Yes, friends, that is our intended destiny. God gave the creatures all that they needed to live a full, good life — including responsibility. We were created for partnership with God. But when our first representatives in the biblical story chose not to live the life for which God has created us, God let them/us go. Yes, God let them go! But God kept following at a distance, trying to find ways to love them — us — back into the life for which we were created. And that is what is still going on.

How is that for an understanding of what love is? There is more to it than most of us thought, isn't there? That is what God really wants to find going on in our lives.

There is just one more thing. The circle of God's love reaches out to embrace everyone in the world, and God wants the circle of our love to reach out and surround everyone whom God loves. If that happens, we will find ourselves being naturally responsive to the hungry, the thirsty, the strangers, and all of the other needy people who are parts of God's family. It will just happen.

In case you haven't guessed, this life that God wants from us and for us is the very best life that we can have. It will get for us the thing that we hoped all of our other resolutions could get. It will not be easy. But it will be truly good and ultimately profoundly happy. We don't have to wait until the last judgment to begin enjoying the good life that God wants for us.

What about that other part of the parable of the last judgment? What about the unrighteous having to depart into torment? Well, we don't have to wait for that either. Most of the real suffering in our lives and in our world today is ultimately the result of our failure to learn to live in love. The lives of persons, families, communities, and churches fall apart because of the lack of love. Yes, worldwide political and economic systems fall apart because the world has not learned to live in love, because we have not learned to want for others the good that we want for ourselves — and the destruction and suffering that result are horrible. Look and see if it is not so.

Does it seem that God is asking something from us that is impossible? How can we human creatures learn to love like God loves? God doesn't expect us to do it by ourselves. God wants to save us to that good life for which we were created; all of the saving works that Jesus has taught us to expect to find God doing in our lives are intended to move us toward that goal. Jesus has shown us that God is at work to set us free from fear, guilt, self-deprecation, and all of the other bondages of our lives. God is at work to equip us with the desire and enablement to move out into the real world where we are to live the life of love. God is trying to love us into the ability to love as God loves. Are you willing to let that kind of salvation happen in your life?

Go home now and look under your Christmas tree. I suspect that there is another gift there that you have overlooked. It is a gift from God. It is the gift of life and love. Unwrap that gift and have a happy new year.

God Is Trying to Tell You Something

He was in the world, and the world came into being through him; yet the world did not know him. He came to what was his own, and his own people did not accept him. But to all who received him, who believed in his name, he gave power to become children of God, who were born, not of blood or of the will of the flesh or of the will of man, but of God. And the Word became flesh and lived among us, and we have seen his glory, the glory as of a father's only son, full of grace and truth. (John testified to him and cried out, "This was he of whom I said, 'He who comes after me ranks ahead of me because he was before me.' ") From his fullness we have all received, grace upon grace. The law indeed was given through Moses; grace and truth came through Jesus Christ. No one has ever seen God. It is God the only Son, who is close to the Father's heart, who has made him known.

God is trying to tell you something. God must be. Why else would John call Jesus the Word? That is what you use words for, isn't it? Actually, John borrowed some of the most sophisticated concepts from the Greek and Hebrew philosophy of his day to write an introduction to his telling of the story of the life and work of Jesus. He used those concepts to relate that story to the eternal reality of God. When all is said and done, John is telling us that God uses the life and work of Jesus to tell us something we need to know. What is it that God is trying to tell us?

God is telling us the answer to a big question that we all ask and we all answer in one way or another. It is a very important question, because the answer we discover, choose, or stumble into will determine how we put our lives together. We come into this world asking that question and we keep asking until we come up with an answer. However, we ask it at such a deep level in our lives that we seldom actually ever put it into words.

If we were to try to intentionally put that question into words, it would probably come out something like this: "Just what is life all about anyway?" "Just what is all of that out there that I keep bumping up against every time I walk out my door?" "Who or what is that great big other that I keep dancing with as I try to live my life?" "Is it something good or something dangerous? Is it something that likes me or something that doesn't? Or is it just a random accumulation of meaningless accidents totally indifferent to me?" Do you ever remember asking that question consciously? Maybe you have and maybe you haven't. But you have come up with some kind of an answer — or maybe a series of answers — to it. Just as you may never put your question into words, so you may never put your answer into words. But the way in which you live your life can tell you what your answer has been.

Now, let's pause and think for a while about the things you have seen in the lives of other people and the things you have experienced in your own life that tell us about the different ways in which a person can put a life together. People really have come up with lots of different ways of putting their lives together, haven't they, haven't we? Some have put their lives together in ways that have made them miserable and destructive. It can make all the difference in the quality of the life that a person lives and the impact that life will have on the lives of others. Think about the things you have already learned about that. This really is a big question, isn't it?

There is something God wants us to know. God wants us to know that there really is someone very special who keeps coming to meet us in and through all of the experiences of life and requires us to dance. It is not some random collection of meaningless accidents. It is the awesome reality of God. We need to know that. And we need to know who that God is and what that God is like and how God relates to us and how we should respond to God. Can you see how the answers to those questions can shape your life?

John tells us that God was at work in Jesus, and in the things that happened in his life, to make God known. God knew that it would not be enough to just give us information about God. There were already volumes of written information about God. The Hebrew people had the books called the law and the prophets, and those books contained lots of good information about God. But God knows that we need a different kind of knowledge. We need the kind of knowledge that comes from experiencing the beauty of a sunrise, seeing the tragedy of a war, or experiencing a relationship with someone who loves us. That is the kind of knowledge we need. We don't need to know *about* God. We need to *know* God.

So God did something very special. God sent one who was an aspect of God's own being to live among us. John called that one "the Word." John also called that one "the only Son who is close to the Father's heart." John said, "And the Word became flesh and lived among us, and we have seen his glory, the glory as of a father's only son." John also said, "No one has ever seen God. It is God the only Son who is close to the Father's heart, who has made him known." God is trying to tell us something.

What is God trying to tell us? I have already said that what we need to know cannot be summed up in information. But that is all I have at my disposal right now. So let me suggest two ways in which you can get the picture.

The first is to look at the event that was the life of Christ as a whole and ask "What is its significance?" The life of

Jesus was a real event in the history of the world. We are accustomed to asking the significance of events. The people who believe that the life of Jesus is a significant event have given us some summaries. They may be familiar to you.

> For God so loved the world that he gave his only Son, so that everyone who believes in him may not perish but may have eternal life. Indeed, God did not send the Son into the world to condemn the world, but in order that the world might be saved through him.
> (John 3:16-17)

If you can take that in, it can make a big difference in your life. Think what it would mean to believe that the one who comes to meet us in life inviting us to dance is someone who loves us, someone who wants life at its best for us, someone who has made a costly commitment to saving us from the messes we keep making of our lives, someone who comes to lead us to the fulfillment of our own highest possibilities. If we can really believe that, it can make a big difference in the way we go to meet life, couldn't it?

There is an even better way of hearing what God wants to tell us. Read the story that John tells. Read the stories that Matthew, Mark, and Luke tell too. Read them as if they were really written to you. When you read something that Jesus said, assume that he said it to you. When you read about Jesus having some kind of an interaction with some other person in the story, put yourself in the place of that other person and read the story as if Jesus were having that inter-action with you. That can be a really exciting thing to do. There is a story in the third chapter of John's gospel about a conversation Jesus had with a respected old Pharisee named Nicodemus (John 3:1-21). Jesus wound up saying to him, "You must be born from above." It was a way of saying that even though you are living a good and respectable life, you need to start over and let God put it together for you in an entirely different way. Can you imagine yourself having that kind of a conversation with Jesus? In the next chapter, there is a story in which Jesus has a conversation with a woman who has messed her life up so badly that she is ashamed to go to the town well to draw water when the other women are there (John 4:1-30). That is kind of a stormy conversation, but it ends with Jesus showing the woman that there is another possibility for her, a better one. In the eighth chapter, there is a story about Jesus forgiving a woman who was guilty of adultery and shaming the proud people who wanted to stone her to death for it (John 8:1-11). Where might you fit into that story?

Then as the story comes to its climax, stand and watch Jesus suffering on the cross and know that it was done for you. Stand with the disciples as they discover that Jesus is still alive and life is full of God-given possibilities for you as for them.

Read the story and let it be for you an interpretation of the things that are going on in your own life.

Can you imagine the difference believing those things can make in your life? Oh, they might not make much difference if you think of them as information about some remote deity who lives on the other side of the sky. If you can believe that they are telling you the truth about the one who comes to meet you and interact with you in every interaction and experience and relationship of your daily life, it can make a huge difference. It can give new meaning to your life. It can fill your life with new possibilities and make it into a real adventure. It may bring new requirements to your life, but it will also bring new gifts as well. There is no way in which I can tell you all that it can mean. You will have to make the discoveries as you undertake the adventure.

Of course, all of that depends upon your being able to believe that the things Jesus has shown us are the truth about the God who meets us in life. Let's admit it. It is not always easy for us to believe. There are lots of things happening in our lives that may make us wonder how they could be parts of the good gift of a loving God. Back during the last century, there was a philosopher named Albert Camus who was in the French underground during the Nazi occupation of his country. He experienced so much cruelty and suffering that he came out believing that, if there is a God, God must be a murderer. When you consider what he had experienced, you can understand why he thought that way.

Believing is always a risky business. It always involves taking an honest look at all that is before you, making allowances for the exceptions, and then making a courageous decision to bet your life on the beliefs that you have chosen to allow to shape your life. It has been reported that, late in his life, Albert Camus had fresh exposure to the Christian faith and was able to see things differently. Can you bet your life on the belief that Jesus really has told us what we need to know about God and about life?

There have always been those who could not believe it. John tells us that Jesus "came to what was his own, and his own people did not accept him. But to all who received him, who believed in his name, he gave power to become children of God..." (John 11-12).

A certain man has told the story of how this worked out for him. Fred chose to let the wrong set of beliefs shape his life. He had grown up hearing the story of Jesus, but he chose to let our materialistic culture tell him what life is all about. Fred was an ambitious young man. Even before he finished high school, he knew that he wanted to succeed in business and to prosper. He worked hard at doing that. At a very early age, his efforts paid dividends. He established a profitable business and then another and another. At a very early age, he had all of the things he had hoped for. He married his high school sweetheart. They had a fine house and expensive cars. Since he was known as a successful young man, he was accepted as a leader in his community. He was asked to be a leader in his church, even though his faith did not really mean much to him. From the outside, Fred's life looked great.

Evidently something important was missing. He began to drink heavily. He began to neglect his business and his relationships. Eventually things began to fall apart; his business, his family, his life. He lost all of the things that had been so important to him. He was reduced to making a living by playing guitar in a nightclub. That made it easier to sink deeper into his alcohol abuse. He was near the end of his possibilities.

Then one day an old friend who still cared for him persuaded him to go with him on a religious retreat. There he heard other people like himself talking about the religious faith that he had professed but not taken seriously. They told how that faith was making a difference in their lives. Fred decided to give it a try. He moved the things that he had heard about Jesus from the periphery of his life to the center. He let those things lead him into a new, life-shaping relationship with the living God. He discovered a new meaning in life. He recovered his personhood. Bit by bit that relationship with God began to reshape his life from the inside out. He had been given the power to become a child of God.

That same possibility is before you. God is trying to tell you something. Can you believe it?

Humanity Reaching Out

In the time of King Herod, after Jesus was born in Bethlehem of Judea, wise men from the East came to Jerusalem, asking, "Where is the child who has been born king of the Jews? For we observed his star at its rising, and have come to pay him homage." When King Herod heard this, he was frightened, and all Jerusalem with him; and calling together all the chief priests and scribes of the people, he inquired of them where the Messiah was to be born. They told him, "In Bethlehem of Judea; for so it has been written by the prophet: 'And you, Bethlehem, in the land of Judah, are by no means least among the rulers of Judah; for from you shall come a ruler who is to shepherd my people Israel.' " Then Herod secretly called for the wise men and learned from them the exact time when the star had appeared. Then he sent them to Bethlehem, saying, "Go and search diligently for the child; and when you have found him, bring me word so that I may also go and pay him homage." When they had heard the king, they set out; and there, ahead of them, went the star that they had seen at its rising, until it stopped over the place where the child was. When they saw that the star had stopped, they were overwhelmed with joy. On entering the house, they saw the child with Mary his mother; and they knelt down and paid him homage. Then, opening their treasure chests, they offered him gifts of gold, frankincense, and myrrh. And having been warned in a dream not to return to Herod, they left for their own country by another road.

There is a humanity that lives within us and among us that is always responsive to the showing forth of God whenever and wherever it happens. It is in the response of our humanity to the showing forth of God that fullness of life emerges.

But there is also an inhumanity that lives among us — and sometimes within us — that pays no attention to God and that works to stifle real humanity wherever it lives. It also stifles life.

We live our lives, and the world lives out its history, in the conflict between humanity and inhumanity. You know that, don't you? That conflict is dramatized in an awesome and awful way in the scripture lessons that we have today.

The coming of the wise men represented humanity responding to the showing forth of God. Can you visualize the commotion the Magi must have caused, richly dressed travelers with a whole caravan of attendants riding into the dusty working folk's neighborhood of Bethlehem, looking for someone whom they said would be a king? Even if the people had forgotten the special things that happened on the night of the baby's birth, that must have filled them all with wonder.

Who are these strange travelers looking for Jesus? They must have seemed to Mary and Joseph and to the people of Bethlehem to be visitors from another world, and in fact they were. Some of our Christmas cards and other traditions picture them as three people who represent the three major racial groups that make up the world's population as we know it. That is probably not historically accurate, but it is a meaningful interpretation of the message of the story. They were probably from Persia, seers trained in astrology, adherents to the Zoroastrian religion, maybe advisors to the rulers of Persia. These wise men represent the rest of the world. They represent humanity in us and in our world that is always reaching out to humanity, wherever it is across all of the boundaries that would divide us, in an effort to pull the world together and make it good.

It is that humanity that reverences life, beauty, and hope. It is the implanted image of the loving God that is in us and in our world. It is through humanity that God reaches out to work in our lives and in our world to save us to the life for which we were created.

This story helps us put the Christmas message in its larger context. The story of God's saving work as we have it takes place mostly within a Jewish world and within the Christian community that developed within that world. It needed to happen in some particular time and place so that we can understand it. But we who live in a bigger world need to be reminded that the things happening within that story have to do with the whole creation. The love of God and the saving work of God are for everyone. The writer of the letter to the Ephesians recognized that when he wrote:

> With all wisdom and insight, he (God) has made known to us the mystery of his will, according to his good pleasure that he set forth in Christ, as a plan for the fullness of time, to gather up all things in him, things in heaven and things on earth.
> (Ephesians 1:8-10)

God is always working to pull us together and to make life good for everyone.

When we think thoughts like that, our hearts are often lifted up by a vision of reality that is full of hope. But too often, right after the elation a somber voice speaks in the back of our minds, saying, "But life really isn't like that. There is a lot of tragedy and meanness and suffering in this world." And that is true. The next part of the story shows it. Only a short time after the wise men left the people of Bethlehem with their hearts full of wonder, the soldiers came and used their swords to carry out the orders of a jealous tyrant. The slaughter of the innocent children dramatizes that which happens in our world. There are still tyrants who will imprison or kill any who get in the way of their plans. There are still innocent people slaughtered in the wars that sweep our world. There are many others who are forced into starvation by the simple negligence of our world's way of putting things together. There are still innocent people killed in the name of religion. And there are also the little inhumanities we commit against each other without thinking, which kill something that could be beautiful in another.

The slaughter of the innocent children dramatizes something that is an all-too real aspect of life in our world. When the soldiers left, a community of people was left crying out in grief and in anger and probably thinking that they would never dare to cherish hope again. If we are sensitive to what goes on around us, we must sometimes feel that way too. It is the result of the inhumanity that always seems to be at work to destroy everything truly human and everything genuinely divine among us.

The Bible writers were well aware of the conflict between good and evil that is always going on in human life and history. The earliest writers thought in terms of a conflict between order and chaos, with God constantly working to keep chaos at bay and bring order to the creation. Some who lived during the life of Jesus thought of the world's population as being divided between the sons of darkness and the sons of light. They thought human history was moving toward a time when there would be a great and violent battle between the two forces. That is one of the great dangers in our human existence. Once we begin to know who we are as people, we are tempted to think that all who are different from us are not really human, and sometimes we feel righteous about trying to destroy them. When that happens, inhumanity wins by subversion. It destroys us as we tear down the humanity of others.

That has happened all too often in human history. As the Christian community grew within the Jewish community, conflicts developed between them as they worked to try to understand what a Christian is and what a Jew is. Some of those conflicts are reflected in our Bible. Paul reflected his deep anguish over the conflicts in chapters 9, 10, and 11 of his letter to the Romans. He knew God loved both the Jews and the Gentiles.

In the history of religions, many of the great religions started as pacifist but turned violent in their interactions with people who were different. It happened in the history of the Christian faith, especially during the crusades. Anyone who knows the history of the crusades knows that it was a time when Christianity almost lost its true nature. It is happening now in some parts of the Muslim community. There are Christians who think they should respond by returning hate for hate and violence for violence. But in that, inhumanity would win its victory.

In the time before Jesus came, many people thought they should be ready to fight in a battle between the sons of light and the sons of darkness. They were hoping that a messiah would come to lead them to victory in that battle. To be specific, they hoped the messiah would organize an army to drive out the Roman army of occupation.

But then God sent the little child who was the center of our story to be the messiah. He grew up to be one who would show us another way. He came teaching us to overcome evil with good and to defeat hatred and inhumanity with love, a love that will evoke humanity. Listen to some of the things Jesus said:

> Love your enemies, do good to those who hate you, bless those who curse you, pray for those who abuse you. If anyone strikes you on the cheek, offer the other also; and from anyone who takes away your coat do not withhold even your shirt. Give to everyone who begs from you; and if anyone takes away your goods, do not ask for them again. Do to others as you would have them do to you.
> (Luke 6:27-31)

> Be merciful, just as your Father is merciful.
> (Luke 6:36)

Paul summarized these teachings by saying, "Do not be overcome by evil, but overcome evil with good" (Romans 12:21).

You have heard that before. Have you yet taken it seriously? I suppose we have all known that one who becomes a follower of Jesus will be called to live a life that is different. These teachings show us just how radically different the Christian life can be. Some have dared to take these teachings seriously and translate them into a way of life. When some have, humanity has grown. One of those who took it most seriously was a man of the Hindu faith, Mohandas Gandhi. He translated the teachings of Jesus into a strategy for social and political change and redirected the history of India. But it is clear that anyone who follows this way is likely to pay some great cost for his or her humanity. In order to dare to really live out the teachings of Jesus, one would have to be able to believe that what he or she was doing was participating in the saving work of God that will ultimately win the victory.

One of the great biblical witnesses to the saving work God did through Jesus describes Jesus as one who came to do battle with the devil and all of the powers of darkness, much as a champion in ancient warfare would. In the customs of ancient warfare, two armies might sometimes send out one of their best warriors to do battle on behalf of his whole nation. Whichever champion prevailed won the victory for the whole nation.

I don't know what you think about the devil. The Bible talks about him quite a lot. I don't know if there is actually a person, with or without horns, who is the devil. But anything that the Bible talks that much about must represent something real. We hardly have to look far to see that the things the devil represents are realities we deal with today. The devil represents the militant greed, fear, hate, and indifference, which are the inhumanity that works to defeat humanity in our world and in our lives.

Jesus did battle with those powers of darkness by refusing to let them turn him aside from the humanity God had sent him to represent or from the loving purpose of God that he had been sent to serve. Read the story. It started in the time after his baptism when he went away to pray his way through to an understanding of his mission and had to deal with the tempter. It continued in every way imaginable until he knelt in the Garden of Gethsemane on the night before he died, coping with every mortal motive within him to keep from running away and saving his own life. Ultimately none of the forces of hate that militated against him and none of the fears that must have been there within him were able to turn him aside. When Jesus went to the cross, it must have looked like defeat to everyone who was watching. But it was a victory he won on our behalf. He broke the power of the threat of death by refusing to let it rule him. He won that victory on our behalf. And when God raised him up out of death, God affirmed the victory. God made it clear that humanity is the tide and inhumanity is the undertow. All that humanity represents is of God. If we commit ourselves to it, we will be on the winning side.

So what can all of that mean to us? If we will let it, it will show us a whole new way of looking at reality. Let's think about some of the differences it can make.

First, ask yourself this: Is there something in your life or something in your world that is oppressing you and keeping you from living up to the highest humanity that is possible? Think hard and try to identify it. Are there some social pressures pushing you to conform, some relationship that is either putting you down or pushing you around, or some power that is ruling your life through a threat or a promise? We have to look within too. No tyrant can rule us from without unless it has a collaborator within us. Is there some fear, ambition, resentment, or old hatred that is keeping you from being the person God has called you to be? God invites you to claim your freedom. Dare to believe that those things are parts of the inhumanity that God has defeated in Jesus Christ. Yes, claiming your freedom can be costly. It was for Jesus. But claiming your freedom can open the door to a new life.

Then ask yourself what conflicts are working in your life right now. Are there conflicts with other people? Are there conflicts with some of the structures of life within which you have to live: school, job, family, economic system? Are there unresolved conflicts within yourself? Take some time to identify those conflicts. Now ask yourself: "What would it mean for me to try to resolve those conflicts in the ways that Jesus taught us, applying the strategies of love, refusing to be overcome by evil but overcoming evil with good?" Think about that. You don't have to answer right now. This is something for you to take home and think about while you are trying to go to sleep tonight. But think seriously about it. This is your way of participating in the work of humanity to overcome inhumanity.

Here is a question that is even harder to think about. What are the most threatening conflicts that our nation is involved in right now? What would it mean for our nation to apply the teachings of Jesus as we try to resolve those conflicts? Would you be willing for our country to do that? If you have already answered, you didn't think very seriously about it. There is no easy answer to that question. Yet it is in the willingness of citizens to think through that possibility and act on it as best they can that the world's hope for peace resides.

When the wise men came following the star, they represented all that is truly human in our world responding to the showing forth of God so that fullness of life can emerge among us. What is your humanity calling you to do in response to the showing forth of God?

What Was That All About?

Then Jesus came from Galilee to John at the Jordan, to be baptized by him. John would have prevented him, saying, "I need to be baptized by you, and do you come to me?" But Jesus answered him, "Let it be so now; for it is proper for us in this way to fulfill all righteousness." Then he consented. And when Jesus had been baptized, just as he came up from the water, suddenly the heavens were opened to him and he saw the Spirit of God descending like a dove and alighting on him. And a voice from heaven said, "This is my Son, the Beloved, with whom I am well pleased."

"I wonder what that was all about?" That must have been the thought in the minds of most of the people who stood in a crowd on the riverbank that day of Jesus' baptism. They came some distance expecting to see something unique, but they had just seen something they had not expected to see and they didn't know what to make of it.

They came to a place that was far out of the way for most of them. But the place was in some ways a crossroads. They were standing on the banks of the River Jordan, not far from the oasis city of Jericho. To the west was the steep mountain road that led up to the capital city, Jerusalem, with its temple, the spiritual center of the Jewish people. To the south was the harsh desert wilderness, the Dead Sea, the enclaves of the radical religious sect called the Essenes, and the mountaintop fortress of Masada, built by a tyrant whose name still inspired fear even years after his death. To the north, up the Jordan River valley, were the cosmopolitan villages of Galilee and the Greek cities of the Decapolis. All kinds of people had come from all directions to see and hear someone who became the talk of the region. Most were working people and business people. There were even some soldiers and tax collectors and some of the religious leaders — the last people you would have expected to travel to see and listen to a dynamic young preacher. But they had all come. They were coming in increasing numbers. It had been a long time since the people had experienced the work of a real religious reformer.

And there he was, John the son of the priest Zechariah, an impressive person; young, vigorous, with his hair and beard untrimmed as was the custom of certain people who were dedicated to the service of God, dressed in rough garments that suggested the garb of the ancient prophet Elijah. Even silhouetted against the golden limestone cliffs that reached halfway to the sky, he was an impressive person.

Those who came heard the message they had expected to hear, an audacious proclamation that the long-expected day of the Lord was near and a warning that the people must get ready by putting away their sins and returning to the righteousness that their faith had taught. For all who came sincerely, John had compassion, even for the soldiers and the tax collectors whom everyone hated. But when some of the religious leaders came whom he thought were just going through the motions of repenting, he had no patience. John was courageous in his preaching. He had even taken the governor to task for having married his brother's ex-wife. The people stood in the sun and heard John deliver his passionate message. Then they watched as John did what they had heard he would do. He invited all who were sincere about their repentance to wade into the river with him and go through a version of the Jewish rite of purification.

This was a ritual typically used when a non-Jew adopted the Jewish faith. Ordinarily Jewish people would have resented any suggestion that they needed this kind of purification. But when John called for the penitents to come into the river with him, people came — lots of people, all kinds of people. The people on the riverbank watched. It was what they had expected to see.

Then something happened that surprised everybody. Another young man about the age of John waded into the water and went up to John and asked to be baptized. Maybe John had been preoccupied with the last person he had baptized, maybe he had not recognized the person who came until the last moment. But when John saw this young man standing before him, he stopped and gazed at him in wonderment. It was Jesus. He came from Nazareth in Galilee for a very special reason. John was surprised. He wondered what this was all about. Those who were near enough overheard John saying, "What are you doing here? You don't need to be baptized. I need to be baptized by you." And Jesus said, "Just do it. It needs to happen."

What happened? Had John suddenly received a revelation that he was looking at the promised messiah? There is another possible explanation. Now we are using our imagination, but it may not be inappropriate to guess that the story may have actually gone like this. John and Jesus knew each other. They knew each other well. They were kinsmen. They probably played together as boys, just like other boys played together. But both of these young men had been told by their parents from a very early age that God was about to do something very special in the history of their people, and they had been chosen to play important roles in it. They must have been very exceptional young people with exceptional insights into the religious meaning of life. We can imagine that they would have eventually found out about each other. And having discovered what they had in common, don't you imagine that a unique kind of friendship must have grown between them?

Can you imagine that they sought every opportunity to spend time together, take long walks during family gatherings or religious festivals, and stay up late at night talking about the things on their minds? They must have spent a lot of time thinking about the things the prophets taught about the promised day of the Lord. They must have known well the teachings of the prophet Isaiah, that before the messiah would come another would come to prepare the way.

They must have also known well the teaching that God sought those who would play the role of the servant of the God, in Hebrew the *ebed Jahweh*, one who would be so completely committed to the purpose of God that God could work through him to accomplish God's purpose on earth. They must have heard religious scholars discussing whether these mysterious passages referred to Moses, David, or the prophet himself, or maybe the people of Israel as a holy nation — or perhaps to someone who was yet to come. Together the young men must have wondered who would fulfill these purposes. They must especially have wondered who Isaiah meant when he represented God, saying: "Here is my servant, whom I uphold, my chosen, in whom my soul delights; I have put my spirit upon him; he will bring forth justice to the nations" (Isaiah 42:1). They must have brooded about the passages that said:

> He was despised and rejected by others; a man of suffering and acquainted with infirmity; and as one from whom others hide their faces he was despised, and we held him of no account. Surely he has borne our infirmities and carried our diseases; yet we accounted him stricken, struck down by God, and afflicted. But he was wounded for our transgressions, crushed for our iniquities; upon him was the punishment that made us whole, and by his bruises we are healed.
> (Isaiah 53:3-5)

The boys must have talked a lot about who might be the one whom God would find to make that kind of total commitment to the purpose of God and to venture out, not knowing where the purpose would take him or what would be required but only knowing that the commitment would be costly — and that it would be necessary for the salvation of God's people. Those conversations must have gone deep, and we can imagine they established a very special relationship between the two.

But young adulthood may have separated the two for a time. Some say that John may have spent time studying among the Essenes. You might have expected that of the son of a priest. Jesus must have been outwardly apprenticed to the village carpenter. But he must have spent most of his time brooding upon a decision that he had to make. God was about to do something really big. The Bible writers often talk about it as if it were something predetermined by the will of God. In a sense, it was. But there was to be human participation in this work and there was a human decision to be made about it. It is hard for us to see both sides of this dramatic situation. We have heard how God, the Word, came to live among us as one of us. We have heard how God acted to orchestrate the birth of one who was destined to be the messiah. If this story of the coming of the savior was not something that God did, then it really can't mean for us what we believe it means.

But Jesus was also one like us, someone who had to make human decisions about his participation in the work of God. Jesus must have spent a lot of time remembering the things that Isaiah said and the long talks that he and John had about it. Was he indeed born and chosen and called to be the servant of God? No doubt Jesus kept himself free of sin as best he could in preparation for fulfilling whatever high purpose he was chosen for. Was he the one who had been chosen?

Even though he kept himself free from sin in preparation

for whatever purpose was to shape his life, he would have to enter into all of the suffering and pain that resulted from all of the sinfulness of humanity. In love, he would take the world's sins upon himself and suffer the results of them. He would stand beside all of humanity in love for all humankind in order to represent them to God.

In commitment, Jesus would have to be willing to follow the guidance of the Spirit of God and to do whatever needed to be done to accomplish the purpose of God. There was no telling where that would lead, but he would have to be willing to go. Jesus had a human decision to make in order to play his appointed role in the saving work of God. He must have spent a lot of time brooding upon that and thinking things through with the very best critical thinking he could muster, while praying his way through to an ability to trust God to enable him and a willingness to say yes to whatever God would require of him. This must have been a deeply human struggle, an endeavor not unlike the ones we go through to make the big decisions in our lives. It must have taken him years to be ready to do what he eventually decided that he must do.

John must have gone through a similar process of deciding. He must have come to believe that he had been chosen to be the one who would prepare the way for the messiah. And he threw himself into the fulfillment of that role with all his strength. But he must have been plagued by wondering, "Am I being a fool?" "Is this really a participation in the work of God or a crazy fantasy?" And "If this is real, who will the messiah be?" Then we can imagine that on that day, standing thigh-deep in the river and looking into the familiar face of Jesus, it all came together for him. In a moment of realization he saw what was happening. The Bible writers tell us that Jesus had a similar moment of realization. Yes, the decision was the right one. Yes, God was here to take charge of the life that was being committed to him. They heard again words from God first mediated through Isaiah: "This is my Son, the Beloved, with whom I am well pleased" (Matthew 3:17).

The people watching from the riverbank saw John and Jesus talking with each other. Then they saw John baptize Jesus. Then they saw them both gazing into heaven as in some kind of rapture. Then they saw Jesus walk away, past the crowd and up along a rugged path leading into the craggy heights overlooking the river, and out of sight — as John stood and watched. Certainly they must have wondered, "What was that all about?"

Now we know what it was all about. Something very special had indeed happened. A turning point had been reached in the saving work that God had been doing in his creation since the beginning of time. From that moment on, God and man — at least, one man — if we will, one man who represents us — would work as one to teach the world to love and bring real salvation to men and women and to nations.

What happens next? Three of the Bible writers tell us that Jesus went away for a time of prayer and fasting. No doubt he was trying to pray his way through to an understanding of his mission and of how he was to carry it out. He was able to decide beforehand to reject some of the mistakes he might have been tempted to make and get an understanding of the way in which God wants God's saving work done. A short time after that, we find Jesus back in Galilee, preaching the same message John preached: "Repent, for the kingdom of heaven has come near" (Matthew 4:17). We find him healing people, making them whole in more than just physical ways, and calling others to join him in his work, saying, "Follow me."

That is an interesting story, at least if you like ancient history. But that is not really what it was all about. You see, the God who was working to teach the world to love and bring real salvation to people is still doing that same saving work right now. God is doing that work in your world, your community, your family, and your life. And that one who represents all that we were created to be, the one who chose to embrace all of humanity in his love and to commit himself to the accomplishment of God's good purpose for the world is meeting you in all kinds of situations in your life and saying to you, "Follow me."

Epiphany 2
Ordinary Time 2
John 1:29-42

Come and See

The next day he saw Jesus coming toward him and declared, "Here is the Lamb of God who takes away the sin of the world! This is he of whom I said, 'After me comes a man who ranks ahead of me because he was before me.' I myself did not know him; but I came baptizing with water for this reason, that he might be revealed to Israel." And John testified, "I saw the Spirit descending from heaven like a dove, and it remained on him. I myself did not know him, but the one who sent me to baptize with water said to me, 'He on whom you see the Spirit descend and remain is the one who baptizes with the Holy Spirit.' And I myself have seen and have testified that this is the Son of God." The next day John again was standing with two of his disciples, and as he watched Jesus walk by, he exclaimed, "Look, here is the Lamb of God!" The two disciples heard him say this, and they followed Jesus. When Jesus turned and saw them following, he said to them, "What are you looking for?" They said to him, "Rabbi" (which translated means Teacher), "where are you staying?" He said to them, "Come and see." They came and saw where he was staying, and they remained with him that day. It was about four o'clock in the afternoon. One of the two who heard John speak and followed him was Andrew, Simon Peter's brother. He first found his brother Simon and said to him, "We have found the Messiah" (which is translated Anointed). He brought Simon to Jesus, who looked at him and said, "You are Simon son of John. You are to be called Cephas" (which is translated Peter).

"Come and see." Jesus spoke those words to two of the disciples of John the Baptist (John 1:39). Scholars have learned that the author of the fourth gospel often loads

81

words with meanings that go far beyond what they might mean on the surface. That must certainly be true of this statement.

John tells the story of the calling of the disciples a little differently from the way the other gospel writers tell it. John tells us that soon after Jesus was baptized, John was talking with some of his own followers and he looked up and saw Jesus passing by. John said, "Look, here is the Lamb of God!" (v. 36). The disciples heard John call Jesus "the Lamb of God who takes away the sins of the world." I can imagine the disciples thinking, "I wonder what in the world he meant by that."

Two of the disciples left John and followed Jesus, apparently at a distance, to see what they could learn about him. But Jesus became aware that they were following and so he turned and looked at them. I can imagine there was a little smile on the face of the young teacher who was just getting started in the life work he felt God had assigned to him. He asked, "What are you looking for?" That probably surprised the disciples. Scrambling for something to say, they asked, "Rabbi, where are you staying?" That really wasn't what they wanted to know. They wanted to know much more. There were questions they didn't yet know how to ask. But it was the first thing they could think of. I can imagine that Jesus smiled and waved a hand as he said, "Come and see." They walked off together. They spent the rest of the day together and that was the beginning of something really big.

There are many things we can learn from that little story. First, you can't learn much about Jesus by following him at a distance. We are prone to keep our distance and try to do a complete investigation before we get involved in anything. Sometimes that is the right thing to do. But you can't really learn much about Jesus that way. Jesus invites us to come into a personal relationship with him and then to follow him into a new way of experiencing life and relating to it. As we move further into that new set of experiences and relationships, things fall into place for us and we learn more and more.

We often talk about wanting a personal relationship with Jesus. We love to sing songs that say things like "What a friend we have in Jesus" or "He walks with me and talks with me and tells me I am his own."

What does it mean to have a personal relationship with Jesus? It is not hard to imagine how those first disciples had a personal relationship with Jesus. They went with him and lived with him every day. They listened to all he had to say. They watched the things he did. They followed and learned from him a new way of life. They committed themselves to him and took the purpose of God, to which he was committed, as the purpose of their own lives. Life lived in a personal relationship with Jesus was an adventure. Every day they made new discoveries. Jesus was intentionally leading them into a deeper relationship with himself and with God. But it is likely the disciples never really understood what was happening and what Jesus wanted them to discover until after his death and resurrection. If we could live in a personal relationship with Jesus, something similar could happen in our lives.

How can anyone live in a personal relationship with someone who lived 2,000 years ago? There are four things we can do that will make it possible.

First, we need to get to know Jesus. We have to build a memory of that young rabbi who beckoned and said, "Come and see." How can we do that? By reading the New Testament. Start with the book of Matthew and keep reading. It is amazing how many professing Christians have never done that. It is as if we are afraid to pick up the book, afraid that it is so profound we could never understand it. It is profound, all right. But it is not hard to read. You can read it and understand it and enjoy it. It is what some people call "a good read."

Read to learn what Jesus said. "The time is fulfilled, and the kingdom of God has come near; repent, and believe in the good news" (Mark 1:15). "Therefore I tell you, do not worry about your life, what you will eat or what you will drink, or about your body, what you will wear.... indeed your heavenly Father knows that you need all of these things. But strive first for the kingdom of God and his righteousness, and all these things will be given to you as well" (Matthew 6:25, 32-33). "You shall love the Lord your God with all your heart, and with all your soul, and with all your mind." And "You shall love your neighbor as yourself" (Matthew 22:37, 39). But don't just hear the comfortable things that Jesus said. That will not lead us into a relationship with the real Jesus. Listen to the other things he said as well. "No one can serve two masters.... You cannot serve God and wealth" (Matthew 6:24) and "Love your enemies and pray for those who persecute you..." (Matthew 5:44). If we sit at his feet long enough, we may eventually be able to hear him say to us as he said to his disciples: "I do not call you servants any longer, because the servant does not know what the master is doing; but I have called you friends, because I have made known to you everything that I have heard from my Father" (John 15:15). Learn the things he said so well that they will come back to you when something in your life seems to call for them.

The second is to learn the things Jesus did. Remember how he committed himself completely to the purpose of God. Remember how he reckoned with his own humanity, resisting temptation and praying constantly for the guidance of the Father. Remember how he represented God by relating to all kinds of people in love and reaching out to them in their unique needs and doing for them the things needed to move them toward fullness of life. Some he taught. Some he healed. Some he compelled to reckon with the wrongness in their lives. Some he forgave. Some he encouraged. Some he called to follow him. In all of these ways, he represented God reaching out. Remember also how he refused to be turned aside from the purpose, even though his commitment eventually led him to a cross.

Then read to learn what the people who met Jesus said about the saving works he did in their lives. Read Romans 8 and experience the life-shaping interaction that Paul had with the risen Christ. And read the other reports too. Here is a key to discovering the witnesses of some of the earliest Christians. Look at the names by which they called Jesus. There were lots of them. Many of those names suggest a story that some person or fellowship of people used to tell about the saving work they experienced in their relationship with Jesus. We will come back to talk more about that later. But it is important for us to hear those witnesses because, as the old song says, "What he's done for others, he can do for you."

It is important for us to get to know Jesus and build a memory of the Jesus who was. That is the first thing we need to do to move into a personal relationship with Jesus. The second thing is this: Learn, discover, or remember that the Jesus who was is someone who still is. Does that sound like a "far out" idea? It really isn't. Did you happen to notice that the sun came up this morning? It has happened so often that we take it for granted. But we shouldn't. That is really something quite miraculous. It is something that God makes to happen. God is still around. The God who made the sun come up this morning is the same God who was made known to us through Jesus Christ. I suppose that in the study of theology there are good reasons to make distinctions between the three persons of the Trinity: the Father, the Son, and the Holy Spirit. But when you encounter the reality of God in the experiences of your life, those distinctions become irrelevant. They are all present in one reality. When we become aware that God is present and at work anywhere in our lives, we have encountered Jesus, the risen Christ.

The third thing we need to do as we learn to live in a personal relationship with Jesus is to recognize him when we meet him. Yes, it is a beautiful thing to meet Jesus in the worship service of a church or on a spiritual retreat. Those experiences are especially valuable in helping us learn to recognize Jesus when we meet him in other places in our everyday lives. But the really important encounters with Jesus are those that take place when something important is happening in your daily life. Whenever you experience something happening in your life that reminds you of the things that Jesus did, you know that it is Jesus doing it again. When you have messed things up in a big way and you are forced to reckon with your wrongness, know that you are encountering the living Jesus. That is one of the things that Jesus did, and it is one of the things that Jesus does. Any time you experience healing — physical or spiritual or emotional — know that the great physician has reached out a hand and touched you. And whenever you experience love, know that it came from the one who "so loved the world that he gave his only Son" (John 3:16). Do you see what we are talking about? Living in a personal relationship with Jesus is an entirely new way of experiencing life.

There is one more thing we need to learn to do in order to live in a personal relationship with Jesus. We need to allow our interactions with Jesus to reshape our lives. That is not always easy. We live in a culture intentionally organized to make us forget that God is still around and to teach us to let other values and ideas and forces shape our lives. It takes an intentional decision to allow our lives to be shaped by our personal relationship with Jesus, and it is a decision that will have to be renewed over and over again. Some of the ways in which we can do that are pretty obvious. When we look around at the things that are going on in our families or our communities, we can ask, "What would

Jesus say about that?" As we watch the nightly news and see all of the things that are going on in our world, we can ask the same question. Then we can allow the answer to shape the way in which we will feel about those things and what we will try to do about them. Some people have made a practice of asking "What would Jesus do?" It may be more helpful to ask "What would Jesus want me to do?" When someone has done something to hurt you and you feel anger building so that you might make a destructive response, ask "What would Jesus want me to do?" When some other person's need seems to make some demand on you and you find yourself resenting it, ask "What would Jesus want me to do?"

All of those things are parts of what it means to ask "What does the Lord require of us?" and they are absolutely necessary parts of what it means to live in a personal relationship with Jesus. But there is another aspect of that relationship, and it is surprising how often we forget about it. It is the question "What is God trying to give to me?" What is God doing in your life to save you and move you toward the fullness of life that we all yearn for? A while ago we mentioned that the different names by which Jesus was called actually represent the witnesses of the early Christians who want to tell us what Jesus did for them. The stories are rich and varied, because Jesus reached out to people in many different kinds of needs and possibilities and did in their lives the things needed to bring them to fullness of life. When we hear those witnesses, we know that God is still doing those same saving works in the lives of people who need them today. We should be alert to recognize those saving works when they are happening in our lives and in our world and be responsive so that God can do his saving work in our lives.

Let's look at one example of how that might work. The disciples of John may have wondered what John meant by calling Jesus "The Lamb of God that takes away the sins of the world." That is one of several great biblical witnesses to the ways in which God works to save. Some other witnesses are implied in names like Messiah, Son of Man, pioneer of our faith, high priest, and many others. For centuries, theologians have tried to use words and abstract ideas to explain to people with inquiring minds what those names mean. That is an appropriate thing for theologians to do. It is their job. But we can only get so far by listening to them. In fact, the great biblical witnesses are actually stories the early Christians told to try to tell about experiences they had that changed their lives. We can only really understand the witnesses if we allow them to lead us into similar experiences. When you finally come to experience yourself as one who has been forgiven and accepted by God in spite of all of the wrongness in your life, you may be able to remember the Old Testament custom of sacrificing a lamb to atone for sins and realize what it means to think of Jesus as the one who takes away the sins of the world.

We have only begun to talk about the new life that will come to those who learn to live in a personal relationship with Jesus. It is the life that we all yearn for in our heart of hearts. It is the life for which God created us. It is the life to which God wants to save us. When the first disciples were drawn to Jesus, they did not know half of what was in store for them. But they knew an exciting new possibility had overtaken them. They quickly began to refer to Jesus as the "Messiah," the bringer of a new possibility. They eagerly went about inviting their friends and kinsmen to come and make the discovery they were making. Philip found Nathaniel and invited him to come and share in the discovery. Nathaniel expressed some skepticism. But guess what Philip said to him? "Come and see." Let us hope for the time when we are so excited about the new life we have found living in a personal relationship with Jesus that we will say to all who will be open to an invitation: "Come and see."

A New Possibility

Now when Jesus heard that John had been arrested, he withdrew to Galilee. He left Nazareth and made his home in Capernaum by the sea, in the territory of Zebulun and Naphtali, so that what had been spoken through the prophet Isaiah might be fulfilled: "Land of Zebulun, land of Naphtali, on the road by the sea, across the Jordan, Galilee of the Gentiles — the people who sat in darkness have seen a great light, and for those who sat in the region and shadow of death light has dawned." From that time Jesus began to proclaim, "Repent, for the kingdom of heaven has come near." As he walked by the Sea of Galilee, he saw two brothers, Simon, who is called Peter, and Andrew his brother, casting a net into the sea — for they were fishermen. And he said to them, "Follow me, and I will make you fish for people." Immediately they left their nets and followed him. As he went from there, he saw two other brothers, James son of Zebedee and his brother John, in the boat with their father Zebedee, mending their nets, and he called them. Immediately they left the boat and their father, and followed him. Jesus went throughout Galilee, teaching in their synagogues and proclaiming the good news of the kingdom and curing every disease and every sickness among the people.

Something new, exciting, and promising is about to happen. God is about to put a new possibility before you. Get ready. That is a summary of what Jesus meant when he said, "Repent, for the kingdom of heaven has come near." That is very important, because it is the heart of the message that Jesus came to bring to you and to all people.

The passage of scripture we have just read marks a turning point in the story of Jesus. It tells us about the beginning of his public ministry. What went before was preparation. All of the stories having to do with the birth of Jesus tell us God was about to do something special. The story of the baptism of Jesus tells us that Jesus of Nazareth made a human decision to commit himself to the purpose to which God called him. At his baptism, God confirmed that commitment. After that, Jesus went away for forty days of fasting and prayer so that he could pray his way through to an understanding of what God wanted him to do and how God wanted him to do it. We think of this as the time of temptation because the old devil did all he could to persuade Jesus to accomplish his mission in some ways Jesus knew would be mistakes. (Many church and political leaders since then have not been so wise.)

Finally, with clarity about his mission and his message Jesus began to do his work. He withdrew from the political turmoil that was developing around John the Baptist and went back north to Galilee. He left his sleepy hometown where he would always be thought of as the carpenter's kid and moved to Capernaum, a busy cosmopolitan community on the shore of the Sea of Galilee, a place where many Jews and Gentiles lived together. There he began his work. He chose some special people to be his followers and traveled among the communities of the region, healing the sick and preaching his message: "Repent, for the kingdom of heaven has come near."

The names "kingdom of heaven" and "kingdom of God" mean the same thing. They represent one of the most important beliefs that the Bible teaches, maybe *the* most important. This belief has a long history among the people of Israel and different people had different understandings of what it means. We don't know much about kings, but they did. They knew that the king was the most important person in a kingdom. His character determined the quality of life in the kingdom. His will determined what was expected of the people. Jesus came teaching that the one who really is the king of the whole creation is one who loves us and who wants us to love each other. That opens an entirely new possibility for all people.

This belief in the kingdom of heaven has several facets. First it is a belief about the shape of the reality in which we live, a belief that the most important one in the whole creation is the Creator, and that the Creator is as Jesus said he is: one who loves us, one who is at work to save us, and one who is always moving us toward fullness of life. Eventually, after the resurrection, the early Christians came to speak of the kingdom or the lordship of Jesus Christ. That is a belief about what is true about the life that comes to meet us each day.

Belief in the kingdom of heaven is also a belief about the future toward which God is moving the whole creation, both in this life and beyond it. It is an expectation that there will someday be an era of justice and well-being for all people, and a time when we will all learn to love one another.

Belief in the kingdom of heaven is also a belief about the best way for us to put our lives together. It is an invitation to let God be the most important thing in our lives and do our best to live trusting God and trying to do what God wants us to do. Someone has said, "The kingdom of heaven is true religion."

Now you have a basic introduction to the theology of the kingdom of heaven. What do you think about that? I know what some of you may be thinking: "That sounds good, but what did Jesus mean when he said 'the kingdom of heaven has come near'?" He said that a long time ago, and as I look around me right now what I see doesn't look much like heaven to me.

The world has gone through a long and torturous history since Jesus came preaching. Many of us find ourselves involved in one more chapter of that history. We live in a world full of dishonesty, moral compromise, and political corruption. Many of us feel jaded and cynical. We find it hard to take hold of any kind of hope, much less hope for a world in which we will all love each other. We feel that we have to follow this world's ways if we hope to survive. Many of us suspect that if we really did try to live the life that Jesus taught us, we would quickly be run over and left bleeding in some ditch. Let's admit that many of us have good reason for feeling that way.

But the biblical belief in the kingdom of heaven never was a naive belief about pie in the sky or on earth either. Jesus came into a world of violent conflict, and from very early in his ministry conflict swirled around him. But Jesus came saying, "Things don't have to be this way. God created things to be different from this and God is at work to make things different from this." It takes great courage to take hold of that hope and to let it shape our lives. But those who do so can know that they are not alone. God offers a better possibility for each of us and for the whole creation.

There have been times in human history, too few of them to be sure, but too significant to be ignored, when people took hold of God's promise and participated in its fulfillment. One story that came out of the tragedy that was World War II is a good example.

This is a story told by Ernest Gordon in his book *Through the Valley of the Quai*. (The book was made into a motion picture and has more recently been republished under the title *To End All Wars* [Grand Rapids, Michigan: Zondervan, 2002].) Ernest Gordon had been a dashing young officer in one of the elite units of the British army. But he was captured by the Japanese after the fall of Singapore and sent to a prison camp in the jungles of Thailand. The camp commander was so cruel that he was actually tried by his own government for war crimes after the war was over. It was the commander's goal to break the spirits of the proud British prisoners through backbreaking labor building the notorious railroad through the valley of the River Kwai. He also subjected his prisoners to near starvation and to every imaginable kind of physical and emotional abuse. The first time Gordon saw some of his fellow prisoners fighting over swill that had been thrown to them while their captors laughed, he resolved that he would never let himself be reduced to that. But the mistreatment took its toll. Bit by bit, the prisoners were reduced to struggling for survival. There was no community life, no trust, no self-respect.

Eventually, Ernest Gordon found himself in a crowded hospital shack, broken in body and spirit. He was exhausted from long days of hard labor in the jungle heat and from malnutrition. His legs were covered with cuts and bruises and topical ulcers. He suffered from amoebic dysentery and diphtheria. He had given up and was ready to die.

Then one day, two men came to the hospital shack to care for him. One was a Roman Catholic named Denny Moore. The other was a Methodist, the son of an English gardener. His name was Dusty Miller. They rubbed his legs to restore circulation. They talked to him about things intended to restore his hope.

Ernest Gordon didn't know it at the time, but the two men were part of a little group of prisoners who decided to "have another go at the Christian faith" not as a way of trying to bribe God to rescue them but simply in an effort to recover their own human dignity. As faith revived, so did love. Dusty explained to Gordon that he came to care for him because he had always been taught that Christians are supposed to love others.

The movement grew among the prisoners as acts of sacrificial love occurred. One day, a guard in charge of a labor detail thought one of the shovels had gone missing. The guard screamed at his detail that if the person who had stolen the shovel did not confess, he would shoot them one by one until someone confessed. He aimed his rifle at the first prisoner in the line but before he could fire it, another prisoner confessed to stealing the shovel. The guard beat that prisoner to death with his rifle butt while the others watched. Later it was found that the shovel had not been stolen at all. The tools had just been miscounted. A person had given his life to save his friends. The news of that loving act spread throughout the camp and inspired others to sacrificial commitment. Eventually Gordon learned that his friend, Denny Moore, had sold the gold Rolex watch with which he had hoped to eventually buy his own freedom and used the money to buy medicine on the black market to save Gordon's life.

Eventually Denny and Dusty talked to Gordon about the Christian faith. At first he wanted none of it. He had long since rejected Christianity for rationalism. But in time, faith was renewed in him. He recovered his strength. Since he was well-educated and had studied philosophy and religion, he was asked to teach a class in religion for prisoners who were interested. He became a part of the movement.

Bit by bit, even under the constant abuse of their captors, faith revived among the prisoners. They recovered a sense of their own worth. Structures of community life developed among them. The prisoners began to minister to one another in love. At one time some of those who had recovered their faith actually ministered to a group of sick Japanese soldiers, because those soldiers were human beings even more pitiful than they had been.

The oppression never stopped. Gordon eventually learned that his friend Dusty Miller was killed just a few days before the war ended. The camp commander was so frustrated by Dusty's unconquerable goodness that he ordered him crucified.

If the promise of the kingdom of heaven could bring a new possibility to the prisoners in the prison camp on the River Kwai, what kind of a possibility might it bring to you?

The word "repent" means to change. What kind of changes might you need to make to enter into God's new possibility? What kind of new possibility might God's promise offer to the world we live in? What might we be called to do to help our world move into that new possibility?

Something Different

> When Jesus saw the crowds, he went up the mountain; and after he sat down, his disciples came to him. Then he began to speak, and taught them, saying: "Blessed are the poor in spirit, for theirs is the kingdom of heaven. Blessed are those who mourn, for they will be comforted. Blessed are the meek, for they will inherit the earth. Blessed are those who hunger and thirst for righteousness, for they will be filled. Blessed are the merciful, for they will receive mercy. Blessed are the pure in heart, for they will see God. Blessed are the peacemakers, for they will be called children of God. Blessed are those who are persecuted for righteousness' sake, for theirs is the kingdom of heaven. Blessed are you when people revile you and persecute you and utter all kinds of evil against you falsely on my account. Rejoice and be glad, for your reward is great in heaven, for in the same way they persecuted the prophets who were before you."

Jesus came preaching "Repent, for the kingdom of heaven has come near" (Matthew 4:17). Then Jesus went up a hillside and gathered around him the people who were interested in what he was saying and tried to explain to them what he meant. That was the Sermon on the Mount, and our scripture reading for today is the first part of it.

The kingdom of heaven and the kingdom of God are the same thing. This concept is one of the biggest ideas that you will find in the Bible. It is very important. It has many different levels of meaning. It is a metaphysical description of the true shape of all reality, and it is an eschatological vision of the end toward which all things move. (Aren't you impressed?) But the explanation that is closest to our front door is to say that the kingdom of God is a way of putting your life together. It is a matter of deciding to let God be the ruler of your life. Another way of saying that is to say it is a matter of letting the things that are most important to God be the things that are most important to you. That is easy enough to understand, isn't it? But it is not easy to do. If you do that, you are likely to come up with a very different kind of life. In preaching the message of the kingdom, Jesus offered to us and to the whole world a special new possibility. We shouldn't let Matthew's use of the words "the kingdom of heaven" mislead us. He is not talking about something otherworldly. He is talking about a very real here-and-now possibility. It will be a life that is very different from some other kinds of lives that we might live.

In the Sermon on the Mount, from which we read today, and in many of the other things that Jesus taught, he was trying to help us get the picture of the shape of that new possibility he came to offer us. We really don't know whether this Sermon on the Mount is one sermon that Jesus preached at one time and in one place or if it is a collection Matthew made of the most important teachings of Jesus. The first verses of the sermon are what we call the Beatitudes. They are almost too familiar to us. We can lose the meaning in the poetry, but they really give us a rather surprising description of a very different way of life. They talk about people finding blessedness, which is another word for happiness, in the very places where most people would be least likely to look for it. Let's go through the Beatitudes now and reflect on them and try to see if we can understand what Jesus was trying to show us.

The first verse says "Blessed are the poor in spirit" (Matthew 5:3). There is an attitude many people want more than anything else that might be called being "rich in spirit." This is very different from just being financially fortunate. It is a cherished arrogance that does not know how to be grateful.

It is always boasting that it deserves everything that it gets. It delights in looking down on others who have less as if they are inferior. The "put downs" this arrogance communicates can have a destructive effect upon people who allow the attitudes of others to form their self-image. That is especially destructive among young people. No one knows how many teen suicides have resulted from that. But the "rich in spirit" don't care about that. They are actually convinced that they belong to a different class of people for whom the rules for living are different. In some circles, people can be found constantly scrambling to achieve that status and constantly acting as if they are more important than anyone else.

But many people, even many who are financially fortunate, are wise enough to reject the idea of being "rich in spirit." And the very wise learn not to pay attention to the "put downs" of the arrogant. How much happier are the people who know to be grateful for everything they have received. Gratitude is a really wonderful kind of happiness. It brings with it a freedom to make use of what you have that the rich in spirit really don't have. Many who are rich in spirit do not own their possessions. They are owned by them. It also brings with it the freedom to enjoy the friendship of all of the beautiful people who are to be found on every rung of the ladder of financial fortune.

"Blessed are those who mourn" (Matthew 5:4). It may seem strange to talk about the happiness of those who mourn. But only those who love are required to mourn. And love is what makes life really worth living. There are some people who will not let themselves love because they don't want to pay the price for loving. Some people are so committed to their own selfishness that even relationships that should be commitments of the most intimate kind, relationships like marriage or parenthood, are actually selfish little involvements entered into for the sake of what they can get out of them. People who are that self-contained could never be moved with compassion for the many people around them who suffer in so many different ways. They are the ones who make loud speeches about how anyone who is poor must certainly be a lazy and inferior person. Their lives are contained in very small capsules.

But how much richer and happier are the lives of those who dare to love, to give and receive love, and to genuinely care about what is going on in the lives of others. Two lonely people in their late eighties knew the risk they were taking when they found each other. But they chose life and dared to love each other and to enter the covenant of marriage. Only three months later they were parted by death and the grief was deep. But the total life stories of both people were made more beautiful. They knew they were blessed.

"Blessed are the meek" (Matthew 5:5). In every culture some of the people who are most admired and whom more people want to be like are those who have climbed to the top of some ladder by pushing others out of the way. People who want to be like them are likely to be aggressive, competitive, and committed to their own "success" before everything else. Yet the text says "Blessed are the meek."

Someone is bound to say that there is a need for strong, decisive people to give leadership in all of the different areas of life. But a person can have those qualities and still be meek. The Bible referred to Moses as a man who was meek, and there never was a stronger and more decisive leader than Moses. There must be a kind of person who can offer leadership because leadership is needed rather than for the sake of their own need to be on top. Certainly those people must be the more effective leaders and also happier persons. Think of the truly effective leaders you have known. Is it not so?

"Blessed are those who hunger and thirst for righteousness" (Matthew 5:6). We are all good at wanting things and then organizing our lives around getting the things that we want. An awful lot of us have organized our lives around wanting and collecting junk. So many of the prizes our culture tries to get us to compete for are of no more substantial value than the plaster figurines and stuffed animals displayed as prizes in carnival games.

But happy are those who want more than anything else to live in loving relationships with themselves and with others and with God. Another word for that is "righteousness." They are happy first because they have learned to want most what is most worth having. They are also happy because God has a way of seeing that people who really want righteousness will eventually receive it.

"Blessed are the merciful" (Matthew 5:7). We live in a world full of hurting people. Some are hurting because they have made mistakes. But many people are hurting because of conditions that are no fault of their own, maybe just because they were born in the wrong part of the world. Lots of people do not dare to let themselves see that. They think it may cost them something to notice their neighbor's need. So they talk a lot about how many things they have done right and how many things others have done wrong.

But there are some who have learned to "cut their neighbors a little slack" when it comes to their failures, to accept them as they are, and maybe to give a helping hand when they can. Those people are a lot happier, especially when the time comes for them to reckon with their own failures. Those times come to us all. The merciful are able to cut themselves a little slack and accept themselves as they are and maybe ask for and receive a little help when it is needed.

Then Jesus said, "Blessed are the pure in heart" (Matthew 5:8). How much purity of heart have you seen lately while watching popular entertainment media? Somewhere we have gotten the idea that impurity is pleasure. But so much that is really important to us is falling apart these days because we have forsaken purity, things like self-respect and family relationships. Happy are those who have learned to keep it clean. When the dirty thought or the ugly possibility presents itself, don't go there. You have the power to do that. Look for the good and the beautiful and fill your life with that.

The last of the Beatitudes call us to bigger commitments to the purpose of God that can give our lives greater meaning and make us bigger persons: "Blessed are the peacemakers" (Matthew 5:9) and "Blessed are those who are persecuted" (Matthew 5:10). There is so much conflict in our world, conflict between persons, conflict within families, conflict between parties and races and nations. There is such a thing as creative conflict. But so much of the conflict in our world is in danger of turning catastrophically destructive. Who can blame us for wanting to withdraw from all of that and to hunker down in some secure little place we have hollowed out for ourselves?

But God needs for some people to venture out of their security and get involved in trying to make things better. God is always calling to us, through the crisis situations around us, to participate with God in shaping human history. If you do that, it is going to cost you. It is amazing in how many forms persecution can come. But the people who respond to God's calling will have the satisfaction of knowing they have made their lives count for good. That is a unique kind of happiness.

Are you beginning to get the picture of the new possibility that Jesus came to offer us? All of the rewards mentioned in the Beatitudes are just different ways of saying that those who choose God's new possibility will receive the new life of the kingdom of heaven here and now. That is a different kind of life from the lives that we might otherwise live. It is different, not just in superficial traditions or in what we are likely to do on Sundays. It is different in the basic motives and values that shape life. It would be a mistake to think of the new life of the kingdom as simply a life lived by a different set of rules. It is not a life shaped by rules. It is a life shaped by an ongoing relationship, a relationship with someone who is alive and active, a relationship with the God whom Jesus made known to us, a God who loves us and loves everyone else and who wants us all to love one another. This is a God who is always requiring of us what God knows is best for us and then enabling us to do what is required.

We need to move into that new possibility to really know what it is like. It will probably be full of surprises. For one thing, it is likely to bless you with a lot of freedom you did not expect, freedom from many of the things that would mess up our lives if we would let them. There is a new quality of life that will keep opening up new vistas of beauty and goodness for us. Jesus said this life is like a precious pearl whose value is so great that when a merchant finds it he will go and sell everything else that he has so he can buy it (Matthew 13:45). This is the truly good life for which God created us.

Well, what do you think? Are you ready for something really different? Are you ready for a new possibility? That possibility is before you. It is always there. God has put it there. "Repent, for the kingdom of heaven has come near."

Epiphany 5
Ordinary Time 5
Matthew 5:13-20
Isaiah 58:1-12

Called to Bigness

You are the salt of the earth; but if salt has lost its taste, how can its saltiness be restored? It is no longer good for anything, but is thrown out and trampled under foot. You are the light of the world. A city built on a hill cannot be hid. No one after lighting a lamp puts it under the bushel basket, but on the lampstand, and it gives light to all in the house. In the same way, let your light shine before others, so that they may see your good works and give glory to your Father in heaven. Do not think that I have come to abolish the law or the prophets; I have come not to abolish but to fulfill. For truly I tell you, until heaven and earth pass away, not one letter, not one stroke of a letter, will pass from the law until all is accomplished. Therefore, whoever breaks one of the least of these commandments, and teaches others to do the same, will be called least in the kingdom of heaven; but whoever does them and teaches them will be called great in the kingdom of heaven. For I tell you, unless your righteousness exceeds that of the scribes and Pharisees, you will never enter the kingdom of heaven.

Lots of Christians think of Judaism as a worn-out, rigid old religion that needs to be replaced. Apparently Jesus didn't think that way. When Jesus gave the teachings that are parts of the Sermon on the Mount, he was speaking as a Jew to Jews. He apparently thought of himself as part of a vital religious tradition through which God had been at work for centuries and through which God was just about to do something new and even greater. When Jesus spoke of fulfilling the law and the prophets, he was calling all who would take him seriously to commit themselves to something really big, something that many of us have not yet taken into our lives.

Matthew also thought that Jesus came to bring the faith of the Jewish people to fulfillment. As he told the story of Jesus, he did several things to suggest his story was like the story of Moses, the great leader and law-giver. Sometime you might play with comparing the stories to see if you can spot the similarities. One of the most obvious of these is that he pictures Jesus going up a mountain to give his teachings, just as Moses went up Mount Sinai to receive the law of God and the covenant God made with his people.

The truth is that first-century Judaism was an alive and vital religion. It spread throughout the world. There were important Jewish communities in Alexandria, Antioch, Babylon, Rome, and all of the great cities of the first-century world. As the Christian movement developed, tensions and conflicts developed between Christians and Jews. But it is important for us to remember that the Christian faith developed within the Jewish faith.

Jesus knew that. He made it clear that he did not come to replace the law and the prophets; rather to bring the faith they taught to vital fulfillment so that people living out of this fulfilled Judaism could become God's agents for changing the world, salt of the earth, light of the world.

When Jesus said "unless your righteousness exceeds that of the scribes and Pharisees," he meant to pay them a compliment. Jesus appreciated the Pharisees, because they were the ones who were taking their religion seriously. And many of the Pharisees had an appreciation for Jesus. Sometimes tension developed between them. The Pharisees were most interested in retaining the integrity of their religious tradition so it would not melt away into the sophisticated Greek and Roman culture in which they lived. Jesus, on the other hand, was most interested in recovering the vitality of the faith of a people committed to living in a covenant relationship with God.

Well, just what are we to make of that? It is important for us to ask that question, because as we read the Hebrew Scriptures we hear them telling a story of a long and varied and often torturous history in which the Jewish people often departed from their essential faith in first one direction and then in another. There are two aspects of the Jewish heritage that Jesus was most eager to recover and bring to fulfillment.

The first of these was a commitment to being part of a unique community of people whom God called into being to serve the purposes of God. The Jewish people knew nothing of a solitary religion. To be a Jew was to be part of a community of people whose life and history was shaped by living in a covenant relationship with the God who was committed to justice and fullness of life for all people. When God first made a covenant with Abram, the earliest ancestor of the Jewish people, he called him to venture into a new life so that God could bless him to be a blessing (Genesis 12:1-2). That gave every Jew something to live up to.

The second aspect of the Jewish faith Jesus was eager to recover is a commitment to the purpose of God for all people. This is the aspect of the Jewish heritage that the Jewish people most often lost sight of during their history. When the prophets wrote late in Israel's history, after the disaster of their defeats by the Assyrian and the Babylonians, they most often called the people to recover these aspects of their faith. Isaiah called them to be a nation that practices righteousness and does not forsake the ordinances of their God, a people who would not seek their own interest on fast days while oppressing their workers (Isaiah 58:3). He addressed to them the call of God.

> Is not this the fast that I choose: to loose the bonds of injustice, to undo the thongs of the yoke, and let the oppressed go free,

and to break every yoke? Is it not to share your bread with the hungry, and to bring the homeless poor into your house; when you see the naked, to cover them, and not to hide yourself from your own kin? Then your light shall break forth like the dawn, and your healing shall spring up quickly; your vindicator shall go before you, the glory of the Lord shall be your rear guard. (Isaiah 58:6-8)

In another passage, the prophet represented God, saying:

I am the Lord, I have called you in righteousness, I have taken you by the hand and kept you; I have given you as a covenant to the people, a light to the nations, to open the eyes that are blind, to bring out the prisoners from the dungeon, from the prison those who sit in darkness. (Isaiah 42:6-7)

This is the heritage that Jesus came to bring to fulfillment.

It is not hard to see how Jesus and the members of the early church worked at bringing this fulfillment. In the rest of the Sermon on the Mount, Jesus taught us how to live in a life-shaping relationship with the living God that will exceed the vitality of the righteousness of the most pious Pharisees. And Paul was constantly writing to the early churches, urging them to commit themselves to building up the communities of faith and living lives that would make a witness to the love of God in a pagan world. Jesus taught his followers to go into the world and live lives that would make a difference in the world, to be the light of the world, and to be the salt of the earth. Matthew has Jesus ending his gospel by commissioning his followers to go into the world and make disciples (Matthew 28:19). Then the rest of the Bible tells the story of how they did it.

The big question is, what are we doing with the calling to be members of a unique community to serve the purpose of God? What are we doing with the commission to live lives that will make a difference in the world?

We have a problem. There is a littleness in our culture that often infiltrates our religion and keeps us from living up to the bigness of the faith to which Jesus calls us.

For one thing, we are so individualistic that it is hard for us to see the importance of being part of a covenant community. We don't like to believe we need anyone else to make our religion complete or that we have any responsibility to anyone else. It has become fashionable to talk about being spiritual people but not being a part of any "organized religion." Not long ago, there was a comic strip about a frontier sheriff named Rick O'Shay. One of the characters in that strip was an old gunfighter named Hipshot Percussion. Quite often, on religious holidays the cartoonist would picture Rick and the other members of the community gathering in church to worship, but Hipshot would ride out alone into the sunrise among the mesas and say his personal prayer "Howdy Boss." Lots of people have taken old Hipshot as the role model for their faith but that really does not prepare us to answer the call of Christ.

Our culture has lost much of its sense of moral accountability. We seem to think that we really ought to feel free to do just about anything we want to do without feeling any sense of responsibility either for the cost of our actions or for the effects of our actions upon the community as a whole. It is amazing how many things we have managed to convince ourselves are okay. That too has infiltrated our religion. It has not been many years since churches required all of the people who would be Sunday school teachers to promise to be regular in church attendance and to abstain from the use of tobacco and alcoholic drinks so they can set a good example for the young people of the community. Now very few churches have any such expectation. Many church members insist that what they do in their "private lives" is nobody's business but their own.

The self-centeredness of our culture has infiltrated our religion too. Many people have chosen to have a religious faith primarily because of the benefits they hope to gain for themselves. When people look for a church to join, they are likely to do it as if they are shopping for a new car, asking which church will give them the most advantages for the lowest possible investment. Few look for a church that will give them opportunities to make their lives count in the services of the purpose of God. Knowing that this is true, churches tend to structure their congregational lives to attract people who are shopping in that way.

So long as we are thinking in this way, we are not likely to be able to catch the vision of the bigness of the faith to which Jesus calls us. We are not likely to be responsive to the call to become a part of a unique covenant community called into existence by God for the purpose of doing God's loving work in the world.

But if we take an honest look at the world we live in, we will see that the littleness in our culture has effects that result in our being desperately in need of some who will come with a bigger vision. Our world needs some who will be salt to give new quality to life in our world. Our world needs some who will be a light to enable people to see things as they really are and to catch a vision of the better possibility God offers.

Fortunately, there are still some people who catch the vision of the bigness of the calling to be God's covenant people and who give themselves to it with joyful commitment.

One man named Thad grew up in a family in which the life of the church had always been an important part of life. He was always a faithful participant in many aspects of the life of the church. When Thad retired from his position as an engineer in an executive position with a major company, he looked around to see what he should do with himself.

His attention was caught by a group of church young people who spent a week each summer repairing the homes of poor people who desperately needed the repairs but could not afford them. He discovered that there were many poor people in and around his home city who needed that kind of help but could not afford it. He set about organizing a crew of other retired men who either had carpentry skills or could learn them. They spent one day a week doing home repairs. They learned that many people with disabilities were homebound because they had no wheelchair ramps to allow them to get in and out of their houses. They became expert at designing and building wheelchair ramps. At last count, they had built about 400 of them.

They also did many other kinds of repair work on the homes of the poor and the facilities of local service agencies. Many of the people in the group were sophisticated people accustomed to wearing ties to work. Two of them had doctor's degrees. But they did not draw back from any task they could manage. One day, some of them found themselves crawling under an old house to replace a commode that had fallen through the bathroom floor because the floor had rotted out. Responding to human need seemed to be the right thing for God's people to do. But there was no hint of martyrdom in what they did. On the contrary, they developed a sense of masculine camaraderie and had a good time doing what they did. The impact of their work made a meaningful witness to the love of God, both to those who benefited from it and to those who saw it.

In that same church, there were some compassionate people who took a fifty-hour training course and made themselves available to help with the church's caring ministry to people who were going through grief and other personal crises. There is another group of men who venture beyond their comfort zones to go into a maximum security prison and participate in a prison ministry, teaching the Christian faith to people who will live out that faith behind walls topped with razor wire. There is another group of people who go to a city park once a month to take sack lunches to street people. These are all people who have discovered that God wants his covenant people to be salt for the earth and light for the world.

This kind of commitment has its rewards. A few years ago, Tom Brokaw wrote a book titled *The Greatest Generation* (New York: Random House, 1998). It told how the self-sacrificing commitment required by World War II caused our country to rise to a level of greatness that it has not known before or since. Those who hear and respond to the call to be the covenant people of God are likely to experience the same kind of participation in greatness.

The Real Thing

You have heard that it was said to those of ancient times, "You shall not murder"; and "whoever murders shall be liable to judgment." But I say to you that if you are angry with a brother or sister, you will be liable to judgment; and if you insult a brother or sister, you will be liable to the council; and if you say, "You fool," you will be liable to the hell of fire. So when you are offering your gift at the altar, if you remember that your brother or sister has something against you, leave your gift there before the altar and go; first be reconciled to your brother or sister, and then come and offer your gift. Come to terms quickly with your accuser while you are on the way to court with him, or your accuser may hand you over to the judge, and the judge to the guard, and you will be thrown into prison. Truly I tell you, you will never get out until you have paid the last penny. You have heard that it was said, "You shall not commit adultery." But I say to you that everyone who looks at a woman with lust has already committed adultery with her in his heart. If your right eye causes you to sin, tear it out and throw it away; it is better for you to lose one of your members than for your whole body to be thrown into hell. And if your right hand causes you to sin, cut it off and throw it away; it is better for you to lose one of your members than for your whole body to go into hell. It was also said, "Whoever divorces his wife, let him give her a certificate of divorce." But I say to you that anyone who divorces his wife, except on the ground of unchastity, causes her to commit adultery; and whoever marries a divorced woman commits adultery. Again, you have heard that it was said to those of ancient times, "You shall not swear falsely, but carry out the vows you have made to the Lord." But I say to you, Do not swear at all, either by heaven, for it is the throne of God, or by the earth, for it is his footstool, or by Jerusalem, for it is the city of the great King.

And do not swear by your head, for you cannot make one hair white or black. Let your word be "Yes, Yes" or "No, No"; anything more than this comes from the evil one.

Once an amateur archeologist saw a man wearing a bolo tie on which was mounted what appeared to be an almost perfect Indian arrowhead chipped out of obsidian. His imagination began to run away with him. He imagined a time in the distant past when someone had quarried the stone from a place far to the north, where obsidian is to be found. He imagined it being crafted by an ancient artisan and sent along some long-forgotten trade routes to be traded to a member of one of the southern tribes. He wondered if the arrowhead was lost by some hunter shooting at a deer drinking from a forest pond or by a warrior involved in a forgotten intertribal warfare. He wondered if there was some other interesting story to be told about when and how the arrowhead had been found. He wasted no time in making the acquaintance of the man in the bolo tie so that he could ask about his jewel.

The man was happy to tell about his tie. He explained that he had learned the ancient art of flint chipping and made a hobby of it. He himself had made the arrowhead on his tie out of the glass from the bottom of a beer bottle. He was proud of his work. But the amateur archeologist was disappointed because the thing about which he had gotten excited turned out not to be real. We like for things to be real. We like for people to be real too. And so does God.

Jesus said he came not to abolish the law and the prophets, but to fulfill them. As if to give examples of what that could mean, he began to explain that the commandments of God and the traditions of the people should not be thought of as just ways of regulating outward actions. They should be thought of as guides to the formation of the inner life of a person or a community. No, the regulation of outward actions is not to be ignored. It is absolutely necessary. But it is not enough.

For instance, Jesus said, "You have heard that it was said to those of ancient times, 'You shall not murder'... But I say to you that if you are angry with your brother or sister, you will be liable to judgment..." (vv. 21-22). The prohibition of murder is necessary but it is not enough. Behind that commandment is the hope that people will learn to relate to one another in ways that will build up the personhood of the other. Anything you do that will tear down the personhood of another is a sin against God and that other. Think for just a minute on the implications of that!

Jesus said, "You have heard that it was said, 'You shall not commit adultery.' But I say to you, everyone who looks at a woman with lust has already committed adultery with her in his heart" (vv. 27-28). Jesus was looking toward a way of relating in which both men and women could respect the personhood of someone of the opposite sex rather than thinking of the other as a thing to be exploited.

Jesus said, "It was also said, 'Whoever divorces his wife, let him give her a certificate of divorce.' But I say to you that anyone who divorces his wife, except on the ground of unchastity, causes her to commit adultery..." (vv. 31-32). Jesus must have been looking toward a kind of life in which there will be no divorces.

Jesus said, "Again, you have heard that it was said to those of ancient times, 'You shall not swear falsely.'... But I say to you, 'Do not swear at all...' " (vv. 33-34). Jesus wants us to be so completely honest that it will never be necessary for us to swear. (Does anyone remember the old cartoon character Popeye, who used to say, "I yam who I yam and no yammer"?)

Then Jesus moved into some of the most radical teachings of the New Testament. He said, "You have heard that it was said, an eye for an eye and a tooth for a tooth." That Old Testament law so many people use as a justification for retaliation was actually given to limit the extent of retaliation.

But Jesus gave a surprising replacement for that commandment. He said, "But I say to you, do not resist an evildoer" (v. 38). And he went on to offer an entirely revolutionary way of working to overcome abuse and oppression. Next he said, "You have heard that it was said, 'You shall love your neighbor and hate your enemy.' But I say to you, love your enemies and pray for those who persecute you, so that you can be children of your Father in heaven..." (vv. 44-45). Now we have moved into something so big that it will put a growing edge in the faith of the best of us. I don't know if it is fair to do this, but I am going to invite you to tune in next week when we are going to explore that possibility more fully.

Do you see where this is going? Jesus is leading us back to those two greatest commandments out of which all of the others grew and through which they all can be fulfilled: "You shall love the Lord your God with all your heart, and with all your soul, and with all your mind." And "you shall love your neighbor as yourself" (Matthew 22:37, 39).

When we catch a vision of what Jesus is saying, we are likely to react in two different ways. When we are thinking of others, we are likely to react by saying, "Yes. That is the way I want the people with whom I must deal to be. I want them to be real people and I want them to have a goodness that is real." Then when we think of ourselves, we are likely to think, "Oh no! I don't know if I will ever really be able to live up to the expectations of that fulfillment of the law and the prophets. I wish I could, but I don't know if I ever can." We are going to spend the rest of this sermon responding to that second question.

It is important for us to get some things into perspective. First, the commandments of God are not some requirements we have to meet to earn God's love for us. They are something God has given to us because he already loves us. Remember, the people of Israel were already the chosen people of God and God had already led them out of bondage when Moses went up onto the mountain to receive the Ten Commandments.

Second, it is God's way with us that he always requires of us what is best for us and then enables us to do what is required.

Third, all of the commandments of God will eventually become promises of God.

That does put things into a different light, doesn't it? Those promises can be very precious promises. A person who knows that he or she is capable of destructive rage may be worried about what he or she might do to someone who is loved. For such a person, the promise "You shall not kill" can be a very precious promise. There are lots of people who really love their families and want to keep their families whole but who know they have within them the inclination to give in to a temptation to be unfaithful. The opportunities may present themselves often to people who live in certain situations. For such a person, the promise "You shall not commit adultery" is great good news. How many soldiers have come limping away from their wars and looked back and prayed, "Oh dear God, don't ever let anything like that happen again"? Lacking some crisis like that, it may take some maturing to enable the rest of us to know that the life God wants to give to us is really the life our hearts are hungry for.

How does that happen? How does God enable us to live up to his commandments? God does it by reaching out to us in love and interacting with us in and through our daily interactions with life. God is always working to rescue us from the things that can mess up our lives and to move us toward the life for which we were created. We must know that God is doing that and be very intentional about recognizing what God is doing in our lives and responding in ways that can allow them to make a difference in our lives.

Start by knowing that God loves you. Take that knowledge into yourself and let it transform your understanding of who you are and where you fit into things and how you ought to feel about yourself.

Then look to see what God is doing in your daily life to save you. Remember all of the things that the Bible tells us that Jesus did and know that those same things are the things that God still does. Watch for any situation or experience in your own life in which something like that can happen for you. When you see something like that, believe that the living God, the risen Christ, the Holy Spirit is at work in your life and respond in ways that will enable that experience to change your life.

If you learn to live in that way, your life will become an adventure.

Do you know what will be the reward of that adventure? A life that is the real thing.

So much of our lives seem to be made up of cheap imitations of life. Have you ever driven into a city on a freeway and seen the sky covered up with neon signs advertising first one thing and then another — stores, hotels, places to eat? And you knew what each sign represented and you knew that some were more expensive than others, but they were all just highly advertised pieces of mediocrity. Are you hungry for a life that is the real thing?

In the gospel according to John, the author uses the expression "eternal life" to represent the same thing that Matthew calls "the kingdom of heaven." He is not talking about a different *quantity* of life. He is talking about a different *quality* of life, a life that has about it the quality of the values of God, the values of what really is substantial and lasting and worth having, values that are eternal. It is life that is the real thing.

Jesus tells us the life he is offering us is something so precious that it is worth giving up everything else to have it. He says the kingdom of heaven is like a treasure hidden in a field, which someone found and hid; then in his joy he goes and sells all that he has and buys the field (Matthew 13:44). Jesus has come to offer us a life that is the real thing.

Learning to Love

You have heard that it was said, "An eye for an eye and a tooth for a tooth." But I say to you, Do not resist an evildoer. But if anyone strikes you on the right cheek, turn the other also; and if anyone wants to sue you and take your coat, give your cloak as well; and if anyone forces you to go one mile, go also the second mile. Give to everyone who begs from you, and do not refuse anyone who wants to borrow from you. You have heard that it was said, "You shall love your neighbor and hate your enemy." But I say to you, Love your enemies and pray for those who persecute you, so that you may be children of your Father in heaven; for he makes his sun rise on the evil and on the good, and sends rain on the righteous and on the unrighteous. For if you love those who love you, what reward do you have? Do not even the tax collectors do the same? And if you greet only your brothers and sisters, what more are you doing than others? Do not even the Gentiles do the same? Be perfect, therefore, as your heavenly Father is perfect.

Stephen R. Covey, whose book *Seven Habits of Highly Effective People* (New York: Simon and Schuster, 1989, p. 132) was a best-seller for a long time, tells of an exercise he sometimes used with his students while he was teaching college. He required his students to think through what they would do if they had only the remainder of the semester to live. He said that exercise often produced some profound responses. The dominant theme of the resulting activity, the underlying principle, was love. Have you ever been pushed into deciding what you really want most out of life? If you have, have you found yourself discovering that love is the most important thing in life for you? Lots of people have.

Love really is the most important thing. But lots of us don't have a good idea of what love is. Some time ago, a psychologist named Erich Fromm wrote a book on *The Art of Loving* (New York: Harper and Row, 1956), and he said that we must learn to love. He said that we need to first learn the principles, and then we need to practice them just like someone learning an art.

If we want to learn to love, the first thing we need is to get a really good idea of what love is and of what the real thing looks like. If we look to our popular culture, especially the entertainment industry that does even more than we realize to shape our ways of thinking and living, we will get the idea that love is some combination of selfishness, jealousy, and sex. Most of us know instinctively that is not what it is. *But what is it?*

If we want to learn to love, we are wise to look to our Christian faith as a teacher. The Christian faith is about love. Lots of people seem to miss that. The Christian faith is not primarily about being good or about being right or about going to heaven or about church growth or about the politics of the left or of the right. All of those things are important, but they are not what the Christian faith is about. The Christian faith is about love.

The Christian faith offers us a rather surprising role model to show us how to love. It is God. Surprise! Do you remember the scripture that left you scratching your head right at the end of today's gospel reading? It said "Be perfect, therefore, as your heavenly father is perfect." If you have ever noticed that verse before, you have probably been wondering what it could possibly mean. But if we put it in the context of the larger reading, it will become plain what it means. It means that we are to learn to love like God loves. It is surprising how easy that is for us to miss. In fact, that is the goal that God hopes to achieve in all of the saving work

God does in our lives. It should be the goal of all of the spiritual and moral disciplines we practice to receive the benefit of God's saving work. Learn to love as God loves.

Then what is love? Perhaps you have heard us say this before. Look at our favorite verse of scripture, the one that says "for God so loved the world that he gave his only Son, so that everyone who believes in him may not perish but have eternal life" (John 3:16). In that context, it is pretty clear that love is a commitment. That is a starting place. But it must be a special kind of a commitment. Where can we look to see that special kind of commitment being modeled for us so that we can know what shape it will take?

In fact the Bible is a grand saga that tells about God's loving interactions with the creation. That saga leads us through stories about how interaction has worked itself out in lots of difficult and painful situations. Sometimes it is hard to see what love is doing in some of those situations. But the first chapters of Genesis are a kind of prologue to the whole Bible. They give us a summary of the story that the rest of the book is trying to tell. If we look at it, we just may learn some surprising and important lessons about the shape of love.

The first thing it teaches is that a healthy love must begin with love for self. That is a surprise, after we heard it said over and over again that we should put ourselves last. In the beginning there was only God, and so God must have loved God's self. God must have wanted for God what was best for God and been committed to having it. But here is something really important. God's self-love shows us the difference between a healthy self-love and selfishness. Those two are not similar. They are opposites. Selfishness is a greedy attitude that centers in self and draws in toward that center so that it becomes smaller and smaller. A healthy self-love is a positive affirmation of self that fills self and overflows in ways that reach out beyond self. We see God's love behaving in that way, don't we? And it will be necessary for us to start learning to love by learning a healthy self-love like that. We won't get very far with loving anyone else until we have learned to love ourselves.

The Genesis story tells us that real love reaches out beyond self to bring other realities into being. That is what we see happening in the story of creation, isn't it? Of course, we cannot call universes into being as God does. But we can reach out to make good things happen. One of the most important things we can do is to relate to other persons in ways that call them into being as persons. You know how that happens. You can remember the relationships that seemed to try to shut down your personhood and you can remember those that seemed to affirm your personhood and invite you to emerge as the unique creature you were created to be. That is the most important way in which we are called to participate in the creative work of God. It is part of learning to love.

Love makes us want for those who are loved the things that are best for them and to try to do all that we can to provide them. Remember how God planted the Garden of Eden to provide for Adam and Eve? God was providing. But God provided more than may appear on the surface. God provided his human creatures with the ability to think, to decide, and to live lives that could make a difference. God also provided the creatures with a person-to-person relationship with God. All of that was important because God wanted the human creatures to be more than farm animals. God wanted them to be, in significant ways, like God. God especially wanted them — God wants for us — to learn to love as God loves. That is really the most important thing. Lots of us who are parents think we know what it means to want the better things for our children and to see that they have them. But lots of us have the wrong idea about what are the better things that we should provide. We are so eager to give children the things that will enable them to move up society's ladder of affluence that we neglect to give them the relatedness that helps them to become strong, decisive, and loving people. Remember that is what God thinks is the best thing we can give.

Love also has high expectations. Did you notice that God put Adam and Eve into the garden to keep it and till it? God put them there to be God's partners in the maintenance and completion of the creation. Then there was that matter of the tree they were not to touch. Some limitations had to be part of the picture. All of that was necessary. The kind of loving personhood God wants for the creatures cannot just be imposed on anyone. It must emerge from an interaction in which both participate. The creatures have to want for themselves what God wants for them.

For that reason, it is important for love to respect the separateness of the other. The theologian Miroslav Volf says there are four postures involved in forming a healthy, loving relationship. The first is opening your arms and inviting another into a relationship. The second is waiting with arms open until the other responds and comes willingly into your embrace. The third is to close your arms, enfolding the other. The fourth is to again open your arms to allow the other to continue to be a separate person (*Exclusion and Embrace* [Nashville: Abingdon, 1996], pp. 140-145).

That means we must be willing to respect the other's right to choose a life other than the one we believe is best for him or her. You will remember that is a part of what happened in the creation story. Love has to deal with that.

Love allows the other to walk away, but love follows. God is still following his rebellious creatures (guess who), looking for ways to win them back to the life for which God created them. God is always looking for ways to win us back that will respect our separateness and bring us into partnership with God. That is what the rest of the Bible is about.

How do you feel about that? Can you see that God has shown us the shape of real love? Can you take that as the model for the way in which you should relate to others?

Some of us may think "that all sounds good, but I am not God. I am not at all sure that I have it within me to love in that way." That may be true. Most of us must be enabled to love. Most people who are able to love have been loved into the ability to love. For many of us, that happened as we were growing up surrounded by love in loving homes. Know this. The eternal God, who created all things and who determines the true quality of our existence, has surrounded you with the same kind of love described in those first chapters of the book of Genesis. Almighty God knows you and wants for you the very best kind of life you can have. God is committed to doing for you all of the things that can make life possible for you. Can you take that in? Taking that in is what the Christian tradition calls "faith."

Know this. God values you and wants you to love yourself and say yes to yourself and claim life at its best for yourself and live it joyfully. God has attributed to you the ability to think and to decide and to live a life that will make a difference, and God wants you to claim those things for yourself and use them. God attributes to you the status of a separate individual who can have an integrity of your own. God wants for you the life of love and God wants for you to live life in a loving relationship with God. God wants you to become a partner with God in the saving work God is doing. But God wants you to choose that for yourself and to enter freely into that relationship. God actually has high expectations of you. God wants you to claim that heritage of higher humanity for yourself. That means God wants you to say "No!" to all who would take those things from you. Know this too: if you ever fail to choose the heritage God has laid up for you and to live it — no, not if but when, because sooner or later, we all do — when you fail, know that God will be following you, just as he followed Adam and Eve when they were exiled from the garden. God will be trying to find ways to win you back to the good life God wants for you. God will always be there.

Can you believe that is the way in which the eternal God relates to you? Can you take that in and let it shape your life? If you can, look around. You will find that many of the experiences and relationships of your daily life will reflect those attitudes of God to you. Recognize them as sacraments that represent God working in your life and take them in. And recognize all of the experiences that seem to contradict what we have said about God's love, for you have come from somewhere other than from God and shut them out. God wants to surround you with his love just as loving parents surround their children with love, so that God can love you into the ability to love as God loves.

This feels like a good place to stop, but there is something else that needs to be said. We have to go back and pick up the rest of today's scripture lesson. Jesus made it clear that another aspect of loving as God loves is to love all that God loves, especially all of those people whom God loves. When love is real and alive, it will start in the circle of our immediate relationships and then grow and grow until it includes the whole creation. God makes his sun to shine on the just and the unjust, and we are called to come as close as we can to doing the same.

This is very important, because it is the way in which God calls us to partner with God in working for the salvation of the world. We are in a world that lives according to the rule that it should love its friends and hate its enemies. Look around. Have you ever seen it more so? And can you see the enormous amounts of destruction and suffering that has caused? God wants to send us out into the world to teach the world to love as God loves. Yes, it is good for us to work at getting more people to put their names on our church rolls, but our real mission is to teach the world to love. When all of the peoples of the world and all of the nations of the world and all of the races of the world and all of the religious groups of the world learn to want for others all that they want for themselves, there will finally be hope for peace. Jesus knew full well how much he was asking when he said these things. The seeds of hatred were already growing among his people, which would eventually have tragic results.

Open yourself to the love with which God surrounds you. Take it in and let it shape your life. Then share it as often as you can, first with those who are most within your reach and then with all of those whom God loves. There is nothing you have to do that is more important than learning to love.

The Cost of Discipleship

Six days later, Jesus took with him Peter and James and his brother John and led them up a high mountain, by themselves. And he was transfigured before them, and his face shone like the sun, and his clothes became dazzling white. Suddenly there appeared to them Moses and Elijah, talking with him. Then Peter said to Jesus, "Lord, it is good for us to be here; if you wish, I will make three dwellings here, one for you, one for Moses, and one for Elijah." While he was still speaking, suddenly a bright cloud overshadowed them, and from the cloud a voice said, "This is my Son, the Beloved; with him I am well pleased; listen to him!" When the disciples heard this, they fell to the ground and were overcome by fear. But Jesus came and touched them, saying, "Get up and do not be afraid." And when they looked up, they saw no one except Jesus himself alone. As they were coming down the mountain, Jesus ordered them, "Tell no one about the vision until after the Son of Man has been raised from the dead."

Nothing that is really very big or very significant is ever accomplished without some cost. Why should we expect that the great and good new possibility that God offers to each of us and to our world, the one that Jesus called "the kingdom of heaven," should come without cost? It is costly to God. Why should we not expect that it will be costly to us? But once we recognize how great and good that possibility is, we will know that it is worth the cost.

An interesting interchange took place between Jesus and his disciples on that subject. It happened at a turning point in the ministry of Jesus. He was moving from a fairly popular ministry as a teacher and healer in Galilee to traveling toward Jerusalem where his work would be brought to a costly conclusion (Matthew 16:13—17:13). Jesus asked his disciples who people were saying that Jesus was. They gave several answers that they had heard. Then he asked, "Who do you say that I am?" Peter said, "You are the Messiah, the Son of the living God." Jesus said that was the right answer and said complimentary things to Peter for having realized it. He said that must have been revealed to Peter by God, and he said that Peter and his affirmation was the rock upon which Jesus would build his church.

Evidently Peter had the right answer, but he had the wrong understanding of what that answer meant. Jesus began to tell the disciples that he must go to Jerusalem, where he would suffer and be killed and rise from the dead. That wasn't at all what Peter had been thinking. He must have had a notion that he was in for some really good times as a friend of the new king. He began to scold Jesus for saying such things. Jesus, who had just been praising Peter for his insight, scolded him for being a stumbling block and said that Peter set his mind on human things and not on divine things. That was exactly what he was doing. Jesus went on to explain:

> If any want to become my followers, let them deny themselves and take up their cross and follow me. For those who want to save their life will lose it, and those who lose their life for my sake will find it.
> (Matthew 16:24-25)

Jesus spelled these things out because he knew the disciples would need to get things into perspective in preparation for the things that were just ahead of them.

All of these things took place six days before what today's scripture lesson tells us about: the transfiguration. This background is important to help us understand what the transfiguration is all about. Peter must have thought hard about those conversations. But six days later, on top of the mountain where the transfiguration happened, Peter got the picture — or at least he came a little closer to getting it.

The Bible tells us that Jesus took Peter, James, and John up on a high mountain to pray. It tells us that as Jesus was praying the disciples saw Jesus transfigured so that he was aglow with some unnatural light. They saw him talking with Moses and Elijah, the characters from the Hebrew Scriptures who represented the law and the prophets. Peter, true to his impulsive nature, spoke up and said something entirely inappropriate. Then a bright cloud, the kind of thing which from early Old Testament days had represented the presence of God, overshadowed them, and a voice came from the cloud and spoke to them.

Bible scholars are still arguing over exactly what happened there at the mount of transfiguration, but the significance of whatever happened is fairly clear and that is what is important to us. There were some things that Peter still needed to get into perspective. By the way, in case you are wondering why James and John were along, Matthew tells us something a little later in his book that lets us know that they had some of the same ideas that Peter did about becoming important people in a new earthly kingdom (Matthew 20:20-23). Whatever happened there on that mountain should certainly have gotten their attention. God spoke to them out of the cloud and said, "This is my Son, the Beloved; with him I am well pleased; listen to him!" (v. 5). If I may be allowed to do a little interpretation, I believe what God was trying to say to the disciples was something like this:

This is not just another rabbi or another political candidate, this is my Son. I am well pleased with him because he has chosen to accomplish my work in the way that I want him to. He didn't take the suggestions that Satan made to him during his time of temptation. He has stayed true to the strategies of love and the

131

way of the suffering servant. That is exactly what I want him to do. Now stop arguing and listen to him.

The implications of that, for those who could understand, might have been: "Jesus is doing what needs to be done and if you really want to follow him, you need to come to terms with the necessity of the cross, his and yours."

When the disciples stopped shaking, they looked up and there stood Jesus alone, saying, "Get up and do not be afraid. It's time for us to go. And just keep this experience to yourself until its time for you to share it." It was important for the disciples to get the message about the necessity of bearing the cross. It is important for us to get it too.

God's love is freely given to us. So is the possibility of fullness of life. So is the possibility of a new world. But the gospels tell us those gifts are bought at a great price by God. The suffering of Christ on the cross represents that cost. It represents the cost of absorbing the destructive results of our sinfulness so that we can be forgiven. It represents the cost of being a loving presence in the lives of those who suffer. It represents the cost of setting us an example of what it means to be faithful to a commitment in spite of all of the pressures to depart from it. It represents the cost of trying to change things in the world that powerful people don't want changed. These are only some examples of the way in which God must pay a cost for the possibility God wants to give to us.

God wants to do a saving work in our lives and in our world. But it is necessary for us to become participants with God. There is no other way for God to make the kind of difference that God wants to make. When we commit ourselves to becoming participants with God in God's saving work, it will be necessary for us to become participants with God in paying the cost of our salvation and the salvation of the world.

Unfortunately, many people today seem to be making

the same mistake Peter made. Many popular religious movements today are "feel-good" religions and success cults that do not talk about the necessity of moral discipline or about commitment to God's high purpose for the world. Many people flock to their cathedrals. Such religions can thrive in the good times. We need to remember that times may not always be good. Most of us in the West have no idea how costly it is to be a Christian in the Middle East right now. The way into the realization of the good possibility that God wants to give to each of us and to our world involves taking up the cross and following Jesus.

Now, it is important for us to know just what that looks like. It does not look like living life with a long face. It does not look like suffering as if suffering were a valuable thing in itself. On the contrary, one who enters into the new possibility that God wants to give to us will live in a daily, joyful celebration of the goodness of the life God gives to us. That is true even when we are doing the difficult and costly things that commitment may require. Mother Teresa of Calcutta was given a Nobel Prize for the work that she and her followers did among the destitute people who were left to die on the streets of the cities of India. Can you imagine a more depressing assignment than that? Yet she said:

> The spirit of our society is total surrender, loving trust, and cheerfulness. We must be able to radiate the joy of Christ, express it in our actions. If our actions were just useful actions that give no joy to the people, our poor people would never be able to rise up to the call we want them to hear, the call to come closer to God. We want them to feel that they are loved. If we went to them with a sad face, we would only make them feel more depressed.
> (Malcolm Muggeridge, ed. *Something Beautiful for God* [San Francisco: Harper and Row, 1971], p. 98)

The kind of commitment that Christ calls for is the kind

of commitment that comes naturally to people for whom something has become very important. Lots of us have that kind of commitment to our families. We organize our lives around doing the things they need. We get up almost every morning and go to work to support them or we stay home and do the things needed to make a household work. More likely these days we do some of both, and we do it gladly because our families are very important to us. We find joy in them. It seems the natural thing to do.

In a time of crisis, commitment can become sacrificial. In March of 2012, a terrible tornado came roaring through Henryville, Indiana. Whitney Decker heard the roar and saw things getting dark and felt the house shaking so she did what came naturally to her. She gathered up her two young children and lay down on top of them to protect them with her body. When things stopped flying apart, she was covered with debris and her legs were pinned under a steel beam so that both legs eventually had to be amputated. But her children were unharmed. It seemed the natural thing to do. When it was all over she felt grateful, not bitter.

The kind of commitment that seems so natural to many of us *is* a part of the commitment to which Christ calls us. But as natural as it seems to some of us, it is not at all to be taken for granted. There are many people who just do not have it within them to make that kind of commitment. If you can, you are part of the way to where God wants you to be. You have received a special gift from God. Give thanks for it.

What God wants is for us to be able to enlarge that kind of commitment so that it will include the whole family of God. Can you get a vision of the whole world as God wants it to be? Can you learn to want that so much that you are able to make the same kind of commitment that you make to your family?

Desmond Tutu was Archbishop of the Anglican Church in South Africa during the bad days of apartheid. He had such a vision of how things should be. He described it in his little book *God has a Dream* (New York: Doubleday, 2004, p. 19-20). He wrote:

> Dear Children, before we can become God's partners, we must know what God wants for us. "I have a dream," God says, "Please help me realize it. It is a dream of a world whose ugliness and squalor and poverty, its war and hostility, its greed and harsh competitiveness, its alienation and disharmony are changed into their glorious counterparts, when there will be more laughter and joy and peace, where there will be justice and goodness and compassion and love and caring and sharing... where my children will know that they are members of one family, the human family, God's family, my family."

He goes on to describe a world in which all of the nations and powers that are at war with one another will know themselves to be parts of one family and work together for the good of all. Many will say that dream is totally unrealistic. But Desmond Tutu is committed to it. He is not an impressive person. He is just a black man with a great sense of humor, especially when he is talking about himself. But because of his commitment, he acts decisively in the service of that dream. He lived with his life in danger for many years. But God was able to use him to help reshape the history of his continent. To him, it seemed the natural thing to do.

Do you have a vision of what God wants for you, your family, your community, your country, and your world? If you will remember all that Jesus has taught us — *all* that Jesus has taught us — you can put one together. When you put that vision together, you will know that it is really what God wants for you and you will see that it is very good. When you catch that vision, find all of the ways you can to help it become a reality.

When you get into that, it will not feel like you are carrying a cross. It will feel like you know you are a part of something that is so big and so good and so important to you that you cannot imagine yourself doing anything other than giving yourself completely to it.

When that happens, you will know you are participating in God's new possibility, and you will understand what Jesus meant when he said "The kingdom of heaven has come near."

If You Like This Book...

James L. Killen Jr. has also written the Advent/Christmas/ Epiphany section titled "From Expectancy to Remembrance" for *Sermons on the Second Readings*, Series I, Cycle A (978-0-7880-2324-8) (printed book $37.95, e-book $29.95); the Pentecost-First Third section titled "Getting in Touch with God" for *Sermons on the First Readings*, Series I, Cycle A (978-0-7880-2322-4) (printed book $36.95, e-book $24.95); *What Does the Lord Require?: Meditations on Major Moral and Social Issues* (978-0-7880-2306-4) (printed book $16.95, e-book $9.95); and *What Can We Believe?: Second Reading Sermons for Proper 23 Through Thanksgiving*, Cycle A (978-0-7880-2631-7) (printed book $12.95, e-book $9.95).

contact
CSS Publishing Company, Inc.
www.csspub.com
800-241-4056

Prices are subject to change without notice.